For the Love of Children

by Jean Steiner and Mary Steiner Whelan

© 1995 Jean Steiner and Mary Steiner Whelan
Book production and illustrations by Regula Russelle

Published by: Redleaf Press
                 a division of Resources for Child Caring
                 450 N. Syndicate, Suite 5
                 St. Paul, MN 55104

Distributed by: Gryphon House
                Mailing Address:
                P.O. Box 207
                Beltsville, MD 20704-0207

ISBN: 1-884834-04-3

Steiner, Jean, 1923-
        For the love of children / by Jean Steiner and
Mary Steiner Whelan.
                   p.   cm.
        Includes index.
        ISBN 1-884834-04-3 (alk. paper)
        1. Conduct of life.   2. Affirmations.
        3. Child care.   4. Child rearing—Quotations,
        maxims, etc.
        I. Whelan, Mary Steiner, 1944-   . II. Title
        BF637.C5S7   1995
        649'.1—dc20

                        95-35837   CIP

"*For the Love of Children* offers us daily entries that are both realistic windows onto a day of caring for children and a light to inspire us to do it so well that we fulfill (the book's message for the) January 3rd image of our children:

> 'Watching us cope with the storm,
> trusting we'd keep them safe...'

This book, with its true stories and gentle blessings, will help us do just that."

—Debra Frasier, author and illustrator,
On the Day You Were Born

"Imagine! A book filled with little stories about daily work and emotions of caring for young children. It is sure to bring nods, laughter, comfort, and new determination to stand up and be counted."

—Margie Carter, co-author,
*Training Teachers: A Harvest
of Theory and Practice*, and video
producer, *Worthy Work/Worthless Wages*

"This moving, inspirational, and sometimes funny book celebrates the work of the child care professional. I particularly recommend it for family child care providers to help relieve stress and to feel good about themselves and their careers.

—Tom Copeland, author,
*The Basic Guide to Family
Child Care Recordkeeping*

To Ruby L. Hughes
who lived her life for the love of children.

PREFACE

For the Love of Children is a window into
the world of people who care for children, who are
part of a broad network that embraces children
from infancy through their developing years.

The experiences of those who care for children
encompass the complexity of social issues and
human relations.

Our hope is that caregivers, whatever their
positions in the lives of children, will take from
these pages of affirmations and stories long-
overdue gratitude and appreciation—that they
will enjoy, discuss, and share them.

We look, too, for the book to raise public
awareness of the importance of child care in a
society dependent for its future upon the love and
skills of those who give of themselves to nurture
our children.

ACKNOWLEDGMENTS

The love of children brings together, in stories and conversations, the struggles, hopes, and humor that fill these pages. We, a mother and daughter, cared for children in our homes, in centers, and in schools for years. We now also teach, advocate with, and learn from caregivers.

We continue to be moved by the dedication of generous, competent people who serve children daily. We deeply thank them and the children and parents who grace our memories and lives.

We thank our mentors who led our way and those who allow us to mentor them as they continue to take responsibility for the children.

We send our loving thanks to:

Joe Whelan for faith, optimism, tenderness, and relentless support.

Matt Steiner for holding our world together in innumerable ways.

Kevin, Sarah, and Shawn Whelan for making holidays happen and cheering us on through good and difficult times.

Suzanne Belongia for daily doses of strength.

Our other wonderful friends and family who understood missed occasions and abbreviated telephone calls.

We sincerely thank:

The Sisters of Sinsinawa for inspiration; Audrey Jellison for keeping us healthy; Eileen Nelson for her faith in us; Mary Wynne for gently keeping our voices true and our papers organized; Ronna Hammer, art director, and Regula Russelle, illustrator, for listening and creating.

And we're thankful for language—the words, phrases, and sentences that allowed us to frame a wide range of thoughts and feelings.

Finally, we send our respectful love to each other for being a mother and daughter who could challenge, cry, laugh, and believe together.

We present this book as a tribute to those who lovingly care for children.

INTRODUCTION

Far away there in the sunshine are
*   my highest aspirations.*
I may not reach them,
but I can look up and see their beauty,
*   believe in them,*
*   and try to follow where they lead.*

— LOUISA MAY ALCOTT

This book is for those who aspire to bring children into the sunshine, who see children's beauty, who believe in them, and who help them grow into who they will be.

The quotes, stories, thoughts, and anecdotes found throughout this book come from diverse sources including caregivers, kids, and famous and not-so-famous people. The connection is in the caring, as these people share experiences, wisdom, joys, and despair.

The words on these pages will stir emotions; they'll bring smiles and laughter and reassurance when doubt assails and disappointment surfaces. Mostly, however, they will affirm and empower people who care for children to know they are shapers and custodians of the most precious resource society has—its children.

For the Love of Children encourages them to pause and reflect on that reality.

For the Love of Children

You really can change the world if you care enough.
— MARIAN WRIGHT EDELMAN

Michelle dries Robert's tears and applies an alligator bandage to the small "owie" he's scratched on his finger. The group of little ones gather around with fingers extended, pleading, "We want 'gators, too."

As Michelle applies the colorful patches, Susie asks, "What makes them stick?" And Jonathon wants to know, "What's this pink stuff in the middle?"

Michelle explains adhesive and Mercurochrome as she guides them toward the door for an afternoon stroll. When Mattie says, "I can't walk so fast," Michelle takes his hand and, at a slower pace, they proceed out into the sun and air and the busyness of childhood.

Each childhood tear you dry, bandage you apply, every "Why?" and "What's this?" you answer, like the safe hand you offer, gives hope to a world yearning for change.

Fear is not a good teacher. The lessons of fear are quickly forgotten.

— MARY CATHERINE BATESON

"Cory, why do you think you can keep swearing here? Do you swear like that at home?" I ask, frustrated by parent complaints and my own inability to stop Cory from using words that a four year old shouldn't even know.

"I don't talk bad at home."

"Well, then, why do you do it here?"

"Cause you don't smack me. My dad smacks me in the mouth."

From you, children learn that there are reasons to be good other than being afraid. They will not soon forget the lifelong lessons of courage you teach them.

I watched from the faraway safety of childhood.
— PAULETTE BATES ALDEN

The threatening clouds of early morning had opened to unload a day of snow and blizzardy winds that whipped the flakes into piling drifts. By late afternoon, people began picking up their children. The parents stomped in, brushing off snow and saying, "It's really getting bad out there."

The center staff helped kids into boots, mittens and caps; wrapped scarves around small faces; and handed the bundled youngsters into adult arms. When the last child had gone, a teacher remarked about how subdued the children were. "It was almost as though they were observers," she said. "They were not concerned, but just watching us cope with the storm, trusting we'd keep them safe."

As they grow away from their childhood, kids will remember in their hearts the warmth and safety you give them today.

Realizing little dreams helps to have faith in having big dreams.

— VIRGINIA SATIR

Lenny could walk by holding onto the furniture. He was close to being self-propelled but plopped on the floor when he tried to step out on his own. Feeling sorry for him, four-year-old Emil said, "I wish I could make him walk."

"Well, maybe you can help," I said. "Stretch out your arms and tell him he can do it."

Emil took his role seriously. Each day he would say softly, "You can do it, Lenny. I'm right here."

One day, Lenny looked Emil in the eye, flapped his arms, and took three solid steps. They both squealed as Emil grabbed Lenny's fingers.

Emil hugged his little champion and said, "I knew we could do it!"

Every day you teach kids to have faith that they can help make dreams come true.

Talk happiness. The world is sad enough.

— ELLA WHEELER WILCOX

The flu is plaguing the staff, and Mary Ellen fills in for the ailing director. Mary Ellen always starts the day with a song for her group of three and four year olds, but she has to leave to take a phone call. An aide takes over, and she hurries down the hall.

The call is from still another teacher too ill to come in. Mary Ellen searches the director's desk for a list of substitutes, picks up the cordless phone, and goes back to her class. The kids are busily playing, so Mary Ellen begins calling the names on the substitute list, with no success.

Reggie remains in his place on the big braided rug, sucking his thumb and watching her. After the fourth phone call, Mary Ellen puts the phone down and says, "Reggie, please go play until snack time."

"I'm waiting to sing," he says.

"We'll sing tomorrow," she tells him.

"Why?" he asks, beginning to cry, "Aren't you happy today?"

Appearing happy isn't easy when your world is sad, but you do it well for kids whose happiness depends on the time they spend with you.

For news of the heart, ask the face.
— HAUSA PROVERB

Yuanita came to my house when she was twelve weeks old. Until then, she had slept, nursed, and rocked with her mother, Francesca, who stayed home with her. Francesca planned to keep it that way for at least a year, but her husband had four fingers cut off at the meat processing plant and couldn't work there anymore. He did day labor, but that job didn't pay enough to support the family. So Francesca went to work.

The first day her parents brought Yuanita, tears streamed down their faces.

"It will be okay," I said, almost crying myself. "I will take good care."

When Francesca handed her to me, Yuanita's little brown forehead scrunched up as if to ask, "Who are you?" Then a big, wet grin filled her face. Yuanita's mom watched and said, "Okay. It will be okay."

You bring reassurance to parents and children with your tender heart and gentle face.

I touch the future. I teach! (I mold and create too.)

— Avisia Whiteman

"Mommy, listen," three-year-old Shelley commands, warding off the coat her mom is trying to put on her. With her hands on her hips, Shelley sings, "I'm a little teapot short and stout." She works her arms to be the handle and the spout. Bending, she continues, "Tip me over. Pour me out."

"You know what else my teacher teached me?" she asks. Without waiting for the answer, she swings into "A, B, C, D, F, E, M, O," and stops. "I forget what's next," she tells her mom. "I didn't learn it all today. But I will tomorrow."

Your help moves kids forward to shape their lives and create their futures. With every lesson you teach, you are touching tomorrow.

*I've always believed that because I was blessed enough
to be healthy and have a strong, supportive family,
I had an obligation to care for other people, to help them.
It wasn't something you did as an afterthought.
It was how you lived.*

— Hillary Rodham Clinton

"My dad told me people who are too lazy to work don't have houses," Cliff shouted out when Will suggested a project to recycle cans and give the money to a homeless shelter.

"What do the rest of you think?" Will asked the kids.

"My mom says we should help people," said Roxanne.

"I'm lazy but I have a house," retorted Frank.

"Well, Cliff, do you agree with your friends?"

"Some yes, some no," answered Cliff thoughtfully.

"Well, you keep thinking. Maybe we can talk to your dad. I think he'd listen and tell us more about what he thinks."

"Maybe yes, maybe no," Cliff said, shrugging his shoulders.

One way you care for children is by respectfully helping them to explore their beliefs. You don't do it as an afterthought. It's the way you live.

Like snowflakes, no two children are alike.

— THERESA WALKER

As usual, three-year-old Jessamyn is full of chatter when her Aunt Gen comes to get her at preschool.

"Two new girls came to school today," she says.

"What are their names?" Aunt Gen asks.

"They're Terri," Jessamyn answers.

"They're both named Terri?" her aunt asks.

Jessamyn says, "I think so. They both have the same faces."

Mary, the preschool teacher, overhears and comes to where Aunt Gen and Jessamyn are standing, with twin girls in tow. Both girls wear white turtleneck shirts, red-and-blue suspendered coveralls, red bows in their hair, and white tennies on their feet.

"I'd like you to meet Terri and Jacqueline," says Mary. "Terri's in Jessamyn's play group."

"Hello, Terri and Jacqueline," replies Aunt Gen. "I'm so pleased to meet you. And thank you, Mary, for introducing us."

Taking Jessamyn's hand, Aunt Gen says, "Come, Jessie. On the way home we'll talk about snowflakes."

You clear the path to discovery when you share children's moments of puzzlement as they meet one new phenomenon after another.

Heroes take journeys, confront dragons, and discover the treasure of their true selves.

— CAROL PEARSON

Howie had fought in a war, run businesses, and played sports. At age 61, he had a stroke. Howie's speech suffered, but not his spirits. When people asked how he was, he would lift his partially paralyzed arm and say, "Fantastic!"

He tackled difficult therapy so that he could leave his wheelchair long enough to walk his daughter down the wedding aisle. Later, she had two sons and Howie and his wife, Lil, took care of them.

Tyler and Niki spent hours jabbering with their grandpa. He lovingly commented as best he could.

The day Howie died, Grandma Lil told the boys, "Grandpa still loves you and wants to know how you're doing."

After the services at the cemetery, as everyone headed to their cars, Tyler ran back to the casket. Raising one arm slightly, he said proudly, "Don't you worry about us, Grandpa. We're fantastic!"

You are a true hero to children because you do the bravest thing of all—you dare to love.

Come and see my shining palace built upon the sand!
— EDNA ST. VINCENT MILLAY

Water spills from their pails as the kids run from the water's edge to where Clarissa, their counselor, builds a large sand castle, complete with a moat.

It's a typical beach scene, but these kids come only once, on the last day of a joyous week away from their cold northern homes. These kids are HIV positive and have lost, or are losing, a family member to AIDS. They stay at a nearby camp.

"How do you select the children to attend the camp?" a TV interviewer asks.

Clarissa answers, "There are so many, and if we had more funds we could bring more. As it is, we draw names from a hat."

She shakes sand off her hand, brushes wisps of hair from her forehead, and says, "With each group that builds its castle and has to leave it, I think, 'If only we could fill the moats with money, then the finished castles could signal a beginning instead of an inevitable end.'"

Kids feel your hope, which hides your despair and strengthens them for the world they have to face.

One kind word can warm three winter months.

— JAPANESE PROVERB

The January blahs had hit. When the last child went home, I didn't want to do anything but become rich enough to go to a beach for a month. Knowing that wasn't going to happen, I decided to pop some corn, watch TV, and cut out colored snowflakes.

"Relaxing. Mindless. Perfect," I told myself.

During commercials, I taped the snowflakes everywhere—in the windows and on the walls, lampshades, and refrigerator. I went to bed feeling a little foolish for spending an entire evening making snowflakes.

In the morning, Taylor walked in and said, "Wow! Is this place pretty! It looks like a snow castle!"

"Yeah, it does," I said, fully appreciating my art.

Your kind words, warm heart, and lively imagination melt the winter doldrums and bring fun to your loving work.

Yet even more important than role modeling
is love. . . . Ultimately love is everything.

— M. SCOTT PECK

Rusty attends kindergarten in the morning; in the afternoon, his mom drops him off at the care center. After the first week, Allison, the director, asked Rusty's mom to stop for just a minute.

"Why," Allison asked, "does Rusty try to do everything with only one hand? When it doesn't work, he's so reluctant to admit it and use both hands."

"Ask him what he wants to be when he grows up," his mom laughed. "He'll say he's going to be just like his daddy. Well, his daddy lost his left arm below the elbow in the Vietnam War.

"The neighbors love it when the two of them shovel snow," Rusty's mom continued. "Rusty hangs on to his shovel with one hand just like his dad. But what Rusty likes best are what the two of them call daddy's arm-and-a-half super-big bear hugs!"

Kids who have positive role models like you to love them ultimately have everything.

*If we allowed children to show us what they can do
rather than merely accepting what they usually do,
I feel certain we would be in for some grand surprises.*

— MEM FOX

Ten-year-old Toby crunched his way through a bag of pretzels while I listened to the tales about his day: the recess fight, the girl who got gum stuck in her hair, the "dork" who got a hundred on his spelling test, again.

"How did your spelling test come out?" I asked, nonchalantly.

"Same as usual, rotten."

"Oh, sorry."

"No big deal," said Toby. "Hey, I'm entering the essay contest on 'What's Right About America.' I want the CD player, that's second prize."

Fortunately, before I could tell him that he might have to learn how to spell first, Toby said, "Why not try something new, like you always say. Will you check my spelling when I'm done?"

"You've got it. By the way, what's first prize?"

"A set of encyclopedias. Not worth it."

Kids aren't afraid to show you what they can do because they know you believe in them. Look forward to being grandly surprised!

I have a dream.

— MARTIN LUTHER KING, JR.

I Dream . . .

That there could be peace on earth—that there wouldn't be anymore guns going off. Now a days young kids from the age of 7 are getting in fights, killings, rapes. I am 11 years of age and I mean this is America and I only see vandalism and hate! I say let's stop and clean up and start making people believe that there can be some peace. So please for the children of the world may dreams come true. Let there be love and peace on earth.

By: Alicia Marie Metz

When children share their dreams, fears, and ideas with you, you take them seriously and tell them that, by working together, we are trying to make dreams come true.

I have a right to my anger; and I don't want anybody telling me I shouldn't be, that it's not nice to be, and that something's wrong with me because I get angry.

— MAXINE WATERS

Marty and I each ran successful child care businesses; Marty called me every morning at 11:15. I would make lunch near the phone so that I could scrape carrots and grate cheese while we talked. I understood her anger about parents taking us for granted, our professional friends' put downs, and the lack of resources. Today, Marty called me from the hospital. The doctors say that she needs a complete rest.

"It finally got to me," she said. "People just don't understand how hard we work and how important it is."

You know the value of caring for children. You have a right to let others know so that you, and the Martys of the world, get the respect you deserve.

To love what you do and feel that it matters—how could anything be more fun?

— KATHERINE GRAHAM

Every day, three-year-old Mary arrives, clutching a blanket and sucking her thumb. Today her mom says, "Sorry the blanket's looking so worn, especially in places along the edging."

When mom leaves, as always, Mary gives the blanket to Jane, and doesn't suck her thumb around other kids. Later, in story circle, Jane asks, "Who wants to tell a story?" Mary answers, "I do," and launches into *Goldilocks and the Three Bears*. When the baby bear finds Goldilocks' bed, Mary describes it as "just right" and stops.

She walks to where Jane sits, puts her hand to Jane's face, gently pulls Jane toward her, and whispers in her ear. "The baby bear's blanket has 'suckthumbs' and everything," Mary says, entrusting her secret name for the worn places on the blanket edging.

Looking very pleased, Mary returns to her place, sends Jane a small knowing smile, and continues the tale.

You need look no further than the hugs and secrets, the heartfelt trust children place in you, to love what you do and know that your work matters greatly.

A stumble may prevent a fall.

— ENGLISH PROVERB

Dressed in new shirt and shiny shoes and his red hair slicked down, seven-year-old Matthew practiced. Today he will help give a reporter a tour of the school-age program for the evening news.

"We are happy to be on your boatblast," he says.

The child care worker is puzzled at first and then says quietly, "I think you mean 'broadcast,' Matthew."

"Wow, thanks for telling me," sighed Matthew. "That wouldn't have been very processional."

You gently lend kids a hand when they stumble. You truly are a professional.

If we could sell our experiences for what they cost us, we'd be millionaires.

— ABIGAIL VAN BUREN

It's Friday, and Shana has an in-service class to attend before her week ends. As the closing person in the toddler room, she anxiously waits for two-year-old Toby's dad to pick him up. He arrives, and though he's almost an hour late, he unhurriedly strolls in and lifts and tosses Toby playfully.

Shana stands aside but then says, "You know you're quite late, and I have to leave."

Putting Toby down, his dad responds, "What could you have to do or where would you have to go that should make a difference?"

When the price you pay for doing the work you do seems bigger than the paycheck, take comfort in knowing you're making a down payment on a better world.

Mistakes are a fact of life. It is the response to error that counts.

— NIKKI GIOVANNI

"Joey, stop that noise right now," I say in a loud, definite voice.

"It's just my music, Moira."

"That's not music. It's pollution," I snarl.

"Thought you liked reggae. That's why I put it on," I hear Joey say under his breath. He clicks off the stereo and putters with a puzzle.

Later, when I'm feeling more in control, I apologize to him. "I'm sorry, Joey. Sometimes I get tense. I shouldn't have snapped at you even if I was feeling tense." I go on for a few minutes, explaining myself and a bit about women's hormones.

Joey listens thoughtfully. When I finally finish, he says, "I didn't know grown-ups said sorry to kids. And Moira...."

"Yeah, Joey?" I ask, hoping for forgiveness.

"I don't even know what 'tense' means."

From you, children learn that everyone makes mistakes. Teaching them to have the courage to say "I'm sorry" is an important lesson, especially in these "tense" times.

"Welcome to the spinning world," the people sang.

— DEBRA FRASIER

Rosita looks around at the soft yellow walls, the colorful crib area, and the well-chosen toys of the child care center in the corporate building where she's an office clerk. She jostles her baby, Maria, gently, hoping her fussing will stop, and waits for Elsa, who will care for Maria.

Earlier this morning, with an eye on the clock, Rosita had bathed and dressed Maria for her first day in child care. Balancing her new maternity tote bag on one shoulder, baby on the other, Rosita had hurriedly locked her apartment and rushed to catch the bus.

Maria had cried through it all.

"Don't do this, sweetie," her mother whispers nervously.

Rosita had already visited the center and met Elsa. Today, she greets her with tears welling. "Maria's so fussy," Rosita says, "She won't take her bottle. I hope nothing's wrong. I'll check back with you."

Half an hour later a message appears on Rosita's E-mail: "Maria's had her bottle. She's sleeping like a kitten. Thought you'd like to know. Elsa."

You make the world a gentler place for little ones, helpless in the dizzying pace around them, when you ease the tensions of those whom children depend on to love them.

It is my personal approach that creates the climate. It is my daily mood that makes the weather.

— HAIM GINOTT

Wind whistled around the corners and snow flocked the windows. With the temperature at 20 degrees below zero, we weren't going outside. Instead, we packed a picnic lunch and ate it on a blanket on the living room floor. We sang and laughed away the winter chill on our pretend beach. That evening Jordan's mother arrived, shaking off snow and complaining about the bitter cold. Jordan said, "Mom, you should just stay here. The weather is always warm and sunny."

You teach kids that with a warm touch of imagination life can have lots of bright, sunny days.

If you have knowledge, let others light their candles at it.

— MARGARET FULLER

Jessica and Joey's dad arrives to pick them up. He finds four-year-old Jessica in the preschool playroom and nine-year-old Joey at a computer, playing a football game. Their dad gets interested too, but Jessica gets restless and tugs at her dad's trousers. "Let's go," she begs.

"Joey, we better go," he says.

"Wait," Joey replies, and demonstrates how the teacher taught him to play the game. Jessica tugs harder as their dad gets engrossed again.

"Can you help Jessie do this?" he asks Joey.

"She doesn't have to know everything I know," groans Joey.

"Let her try," his dad coaxes.

Reluctantly, Joey tells his sister which keys to press, explains how to make a player throw a pass and why. Soon their two heads are together, and Dad's repeating, "Let's go."

Joey shows Jessica how to shut down the computer, and they follow their dad out.

"Gee, Joey," Jessica says. "You're a good teacher."

A nine year old never looked so proud.

Children learn to share knowledge from you, a role model, whose candle shines brightly in their young lives.

To work in the world lovingly means that we are
defining what we will be for, rather than reacting to
what we are against.

— CHRISTINA BALDWIN

Lupe lives in a hot, bronze desert town. She takes care of the children whose mothers cook and clean for the people who come to get away from the frigid East Coast winters. The mothers don't make much money, so Lupe makes even less. She is earning an education degree. Sometimes the kids "help" with her homework and pretend that they are teachers.

On a cooler than usual day, she takes the five kids on a walk to the fountain in town. They delight in the sun-sparkled drops and dip their brown hands in the cool water. When the driver of a big, fancy car honks and calls them names, Lupe asks the children, "Why do you think he did that?"

Four-year-old Ricky answers, "Maybe he doesn't like people who are going to be important teachers."

You lovingly give children the tools and role modeling that allow them to work for their important futures.

It takes just as much courage to have tried and failed as it does to have tried and succeeded.

— ANNE MORROW LINDBERGH

Keith, almost six years old, has cerebral palsy. Although he tries, he can't form most words. Through needed surgeries and therapy, he's been a brave little guy and his parents feel perhaps they should just accept his inability to speak. But, Leah, his nanny since infancy, isn't willing to give up.

Keith's dad's birthday is coming up, so Leah carefully coaches Keith each day to say, "Happy Birthday, Daddy," painstakingly aware she's risking his failure. They work and work at it. Finally, Keith manages a difficult "Happy Birthday."

The big day comes. When his dad sits down for breakfast, Leah nods encouragement to Keith. From his special chair, he says a halting, but clear, "Happy Birthday—Leah."

Leah's heart sinks. But then Keith adds, "Oh! I mean, Daddy." Triumph fills the room.

Your understanding when they fail gives kids the courage to try again, whether it's a first step, a first word, a new game, or difficult therapy.

No one but you has the time or inclination to tell you regularly how naturally beautiful and capable you are.

— SUSAN L. TAYLOR

You. Yes, you, the beautiful person reading this book. Please give yourself two minutes right now to copy down Susan L. Taylor's quote.

We'll wait.

Done? Great! Now tape it onto the mirror that you look into every morning.

We'll wait.

Looks good!

Now practice this affirmation and say it each morning: "I am naturally beautiful and capable."

We'll wait.

We couldn't help overhearing and we couldn't agree with you more!

Fondly,
Mary and Jean

We need to raise our voices a little more, even as they say to us, "This is so uncharacteristic of you."

— MITSUYE YAMADA

At a state Senate committee meeting, the senator's aide whispers to the secretary, "I thought child care attracted gentle people. These folks are pretty radical."

The bill on the committee meeting agenda requests funds for subsidizing pay scales for child care workers. One after another, care providers step up to the microphone and point out the unfairness of benefitless employment.

The secretary, a mother of two, is taking notes and appears to ignore the aide's comments. But after awhile, she pushes a paper toward him entitled, "Listen Up."

On it she's written, "Here are the messages these people are getting: Be satisfied with a lower rate of pay and less respect than employees in other fields; be dedicated to our kids; obey a mountain of regulations; and you're not important enough to have paid time off."

She signs off with a question, "Want to apply for the job?"

When you declare your own worth, you give a voice to the value of what you do and educate people who should know.

You whose day it is, make it beautiful. Get out
your rainbow colors, so it will be beautiful.

— Song to Bring Fair Weather, Nootka

Stomping the snow off her boots, Seth's mom, Pauli, asked me, "Why aren't you ever grouchy? You change diapers and wipe up strained beets all day. I sit in a fancy office and sound important and I'm never as up as you are."

Just then Seth, snowsuit and all, toddled his first three steps, grinning and grinning.

"Way to go," I said.

Pauli said, "Give Mommy a hug." Seth did, grinning and grinning.

"Pretty hard to be crabby with a great job like this," I said with a wink.

"I can see that. I can sure see that."

You let children color their days with rainbows when you tend to their cries, tries, and grins. Because of your joy and attention, their childhoods are filled with many beautiful days.

Remember how long Susie's hair used to be? We've been playing beauty parlor and . . .

— DIANE HEAD

Six-year-old Ellen lives with her foster parents Bonnie and Merv Jensen. Some of the Jensen's friends and relatives resent these little strangers; Bonnie's friend Pat is one.

Today Pat has stopped by on her way home from making a portrait appointment for her kids. Pat's daughter, Diana, and Ellen run off to play while the two mothers plan a women's group meeting. Agenda set, Pat says, "I'd better get going."

Bonnie calls the girls, "Come on. Diana has to leave." They come, very slowly. Pat sees Diana and screams, "What's happened to your hair?"

"Ellen made it pretty for my picture," says Diana, with little hair left to make pretty.

"Diana, you'll look like a boy. We've waited so long to do pictures," Pat moans.

"I'm so sorry," Bonnie says.

"Bonnie," Pat says sharply, "you've made your choice—these incorrigible kids over your friends."

Never doubt your choice when you offer children a place in your heart and home; where you give them strength for the future in the warmth and security of your care.

JANUARY 29

You're either part of the solution or part of the problem.
— ELDRIDGE CLEAVER

Roman is a fifth grader with a reputation.
Every morning I tell him to have a good day. Every
afternoon I ask how things went. I only get grunts.
I see him watching us play in the gym but he never
joins in.

"Where have you been?" Roman asks one day as I
walk in the front door.

"Got caught in traffic. What's up?" I say, trying to
be cool. Inside I'm doing cartwheels. He's actually
talking to me!

"I got 100 in spelling today. First time,
like ever."

"Awesome, I'm really glad you told me."

"Yeah, I know."

"Want to play floor hockey?"

"Sure, why not?" he says, calmly. Inside, I'll bet
he's doing cartwheels too.

**You are a person kids can trust. Your honest
concern gives them the courage to reach out and
solve their problems.**

I beg you to stop apologizing for being a member of the most important profession in the world.

— WILLIAM G. CARR

On TV an affluent-looking elderly couple who have just purchased a new townhouse smile into the camera. The man says, "We didn't need that big house since Sharon's gone."

"She's a doctor, you know," says the woman proudly.

The next ad sells paper towels. A preschool teacher hurries to the cabinet for several absorbent rolls to wipe up fingerpaint spills. Kids dripping wet paint reach out to stop the teacher so she can admire their art. Laughing, she skillfully dodges pairs of brightly colored hands.

Jill, who works at the Co-op Child Care Center, and her husband, Rick, watch the ad. Rick says, "Good ad, but where are the parents saying, 'Our daughter recommends this product. She's a child care worker, you know?' Probably more than one doctor among the kids you work with."

You shape the professionals of tomorrow; never apologize for the value you place on your work.

I know there will be a spring; as surely as the birds know it when they see above the snow two tiny, quivering green leaves. Spring cannot fail us.

— OLIVE SCHREINER

Jo Ellen brought a book about birds for our story time. On one page a big red-breasted robin fed worms to her babies.

"Won't it be wonderful when spring comes?" I asked the six squirming kids. Actually, they loved the snowy winter; I was the one getting weary from snowsuit, boot, and mitten duty.

"In the spring we'll see robins and green grass," I said longingly.

"What's grass?" asked two-year-old Lynette, reminding me how young my bright little flock was.

"You're a delight," I thought as I carefully answered the question.

Even when the winter days get long and dreary, you take notice of the beauty of the children in your care. They can trust you not to fail them.

So cuddly and cute, these wee ones take hold of our hearts and lives.

— DIANE HEAD

Michele, now nine months old, had come to Olivia's at age six weeks. Olivia's other four charges are preschoolers who love the baby. Their schedule now includes a special "play time with Michele."

Some days, schedules change to adapt to the baby's routine. Like last Friday. Lunch dishes got stacked instead of washed, blankets on nap cots remained unfolded, and scattered toys cluttered the living room.

When Brian, Olivia's first grader, arrived home, he looked around and announced, "My teacher says she's making a home visit.

"But don't worry, Mom. Not today," he quickly added, and then proudly continued, "I told her to be sure to call before she comes, 'cause if we have a baby, the place will be a mess."

You give a loving example of what's important in living to those whose lives take hold of your heart. Be proud of the caring talents you have.

To be respected, I must first respect myself.

— SPANISH PROVERB

Faith works with infants from 2 to 6 p.m. after her special ed job. On the weekends, she waitresses and leads the children's choir. She's getting her masters degree in education. She's engaged, has an apartment and two cats. On Friday, Cory's mother asked her if she could baby-sit on Saturday night.

"I'm pretty busy," Faith said.

"Busy? You don't have kids. Is it something you have to do?"

"Yes, it is," Faith replied. "If you like, I'll tell you about my schedule someday. You have a good weekend now."

Sometimes you take a deep breath and say to yourself, "I respect me. Your child respects me. One day, you will respect me too."

*If the family were a boat, it would be a canoe that makes
no progress unless everyone paddles.*

— LETTY COTTIN POGREBIN

Esther meets with Julia Brown, a licensing
worker, at the kitchen table. Esther explains that
she wants a home care license to help with family
finances and be home with three-year-old Wally,
who buzzes his trike through the room again and
again as they talk.

"Shh," Esther says each time he goes by.

When he screeches to a stop and demands some
milk, Esther says, "Wait just a few minutes." Wally
begins to wail, "I don't want you to take care of
kids. You're my own mommy."

Julia gathers her notes and briefcase while
Esther stoops to eye level with her son, holds
his hands, and says, "Mommy needs your help.
Remember, we said we have lots of love to
go around?"

As Wally nods agreement, Julia gently taps
Esther's shoulder. "We'll be in touch," she says, sees
herself to the door, and softly closes it behind her.

**Love to draw on and hearts willing to share are the
principal assets in your business where kids are the
consumers and need all you have to offer.**

Jumping has always been the thing to me.
It's like leaping for joy.

— JACKIE JOYNER-KERSEE

Once a month, Marge puts "memory time" on the meeting agenda. The staff remembers a childhood activity that they treasured and figures out how the kids at the center could have the same experience.

"My favorite thing in the world was jumping on the bed. I was sure I was flying!" says June at one meeting.

The next week there is a mattress on the floor.

The toddlers bounce and giggle. June laughs warmly when Cinnamon squeals, "See, me fly. Me fly!"

Some of children's deepest, finest memories come from you. You teach their hearts to leap for joy.

*Sometimes you must choose to give no choice
to children.*

— JOHN ROSEMOND

"I don't have to take a nap today. My mom said so," Billy announces when he arrives at Sheila's. He's been coming since he was 18 months old. Now he's four. His mom works full-time so he spends a nine-hour day with Sheila.

Billy stands in the doorway, waiting for his mom to affirm that what he's said is true. Standing behind him, his mom shrugs her shoulders in a sign of helplessness and whispers, "It was the only way I could get him going today."

"Say good-bye to mom and come in, Billy," says Sheila.

His mom hurriedly kisses him and mouths, "Sorry," as Billy rushes in to tell the other kids, "I don't have to take a nap. My mom said so."

When others leave problems with you that they can't solve, feel complimented. It's recognition of your abilities to resolve conflict with kids.

*One of my friends said most people are so hard to
please that if they met God, they'd probably say,
"Yes, she's great, but . . ."*

— DIANA ROSS

Cassie promised the kids she would bring
seashells today. Unfortunately, her tire blew last
night and it was dark before she got it fixed. So
early the next day, as the sun rose over the winter
waves, she went to the beach to gather shells. The
children loved their treasures. They each got to
choose one shell to take home to show their family.
Maybe they could make up a story about it,
Cassie suggested.

When Davis told his mother the plan, she said,
"Cassie, I know you mean well, dear, but I'm really
on a tight schedule. Don't expect me to do anything
extra at home."

Don't let hurried, insensitive remarks ruin a good day.
Your extra efforts bring new delights to children.
Celebrate the light in their eyes and the appreciation
in their hearts.

So many people to rescue. So little time.

— JANN MITCHELL

Lisa, a Midwesterner, and Letitia, her friend whom she's visiting in New York, go to Grand Central Station.

Sitting on a bench observing the busy place, they notice a young woman and three children. Large, overstuffed, plastic bags spill out from under their small table. The woman tears at a pizza slice, which she divides among the three little girls.

"Are they planning to take a train out of here with all that stuff?" Lisa asks.

"No, they're homeless, girl," Letitia said. "Lots of people like that around."

Lisa watches the kids hungrily attack the pizza, and says, "Letitia, I'm out of here."

Reaching into her bag, she pulls out a number of bills, and offers them to the woman. As they move on, Letitia tells her, "That may not have been a good idea. You don't know how that woman will spend that money."

"I don't care. If I had more, I'd give it to her."

Saving the children, while we still have time, is what child care is all about. Be proud of your contributions.

There is nothing to make you like other human beings so much as doing things for them.

— ZORA NEALE HURSTON

Once a week Connie arrived to give the place a good cleaning. She glared at the kids if they came near her mops and buckets. I told her that children could learn a lot from helping her.

"Okay, maybe one at a time," she conceded.

Each week Connie had a young assistant. I wasn't certain she liked the plan, but I kept encouraging her. One day two-year-old LaRoyce decided to take a turn.

"Me water. Me water," she said and leaned over the pail to get a rag. Down she went, pail and all. Water flowed into a lake that LaRoyce could only belly slide on.

"No water. No water," she sputtered.

Scooping up the soaked body, Connie said fondly, "Hush, hush, my brave little fish, I'll teach you to be a helper, oh sure I will."

You bring the love of children to those around you. The world is a kinder place because you create bonds between human beings, big and small.

Child, little child, how little you know. Hasten to learn as you hasten to grow.

— UNICEF *Book of Poems*

Barry is a five-year-old kindergartner who has been coming to the downtown care center for four years. He's been the only five year old since school started this fall, and the younger kids think he's quite grown-up. Every day they greet him with a cheery, "Barry's here."

This week Matt, another kindergartner, arrived. Despite the teacher's efforts to convince Barry to make him feel welcome, Barry ignores Matt. Today, however, Matt was pushing a large dump truck along the floor in the playroom. Barry walked over, put his foot out, stopped the truck, and said, "You can't play with that unless I say so."

Matt continued to push the truck. Barry stopped it again and bullied Matt into a tugging match. Over his protest, "I'm biggest, and I'm boss!" the teacher led Barry to a quiet corner to talk about how he's going to solve his problem. Behind them she left Matt leading the kids in a game of "Simon Says."

You help kids meet the challenges of growing up each time you guide them through a hard-to-learn lesson in living.

'Tis the human touch in this world that counts.

— SPENCER MICHAEL FREE

Jillian put the baby, Shawna, in the middle of the room on a quilt. Children stopped occasionally to touch her fingers or talk baby talk.

When they gave her attention, Shawna's arms and legs windmilled in the air. Pete, the ever-observant seven year old, asked, "Do we charge her battery or what?"

From very early on children learn from you that a touch of attention and love brings out the best in all of us.

*In what other profession do you get hugs
each day for being there?*

— PATRICIA WILLIS

Liza returns from a directors' meeting on staff morale. She thinks about the endless stories she heard about the downers caregivers have to combat, especially Jeff's story.

"I had to work at keeping staff last week," Jeff had said, "because some parents grumbled so much about the six paid holidays a year we close for—people who have jobs where they get many more paid days off.

"I lost one person. She told a parent, 'What I'm hearing is that you don't value what I do. I'm not worth paid time off, and it's all right that I get less than you would accept from any employer. That's really sad!' Then she quit."

Opening her office door, Liza's eyes fall on a bulletin board quote, "A hug is a great gift—one size fits all, and it's easy to exchange."

It brings a smile and aloud she says, "I guess I'll stay."

Kids are fortunate that you see your work as a hug above what less meaningful jobs might pay.

Love and a cough
cannot be concealed.
Even a small cough
Even a small love.

— Ann Sexton

Clearing my throat didn't help.

"I'm sorry," I told the story time circle. "I can't read to you today. I have a frog in my throat."

That night I went to bed early with a steamer running in my room and a wool sock wrapped around my neck, just like my grandma told me. I was just dozing off when the phone rang.

"Hello," I said with a sandpaper tone.

"Oh, Reet, you sound terrible," Henry's mother said. "But could you tell Henry that you don't really have a frog in your throat? He keeps crying that you won't be able to talk again because the frog won't be able to get out."

"Sure, I'll talk to him."

"Thanks, and get well soon."

"If I don't croak," I laughed, as I waited for Henry to get to the phone.

Children, no matter how small, give you their love, their concern, and some good laughs, even when you're a little down.

When we show partiality and prejudice,
we are setting examples for our children.

— MARY BECKWITH

Driving home, Cassie, a third-grade teacher, listens to a talk radio show. A woman caller identifying herself as African-American says, "I want to thank a little boy. Today when I passed him and a girl, both about five, the girl said, 'I don't like black people. My grandma says they eat people.' The boy retorted, 'Grandmas can be wrong, you know.'"

Cassie turns down the volume and recalls when she was eight years old and in a new school, thirty years ago. A classmate had told her teacher, "My grandma says I don't have to be nice to her because she's different."

"Share this book with your grandmother," the teacher had said.

The book displayed photos of beautiful things, from raindrops on pussy willows to bridal dresses and puppies in shop windows. A child narrated it, saying, "I like . . . rain . . . pretty dresses . . . puppies."

The last photo was of the child, a wistfully sad African-American girl of about eight. Its caption read, "I wonder why some people don't like me."

You combat generations of harm and teach needed lessons when you embrace all children in the human rainbow.

Love is something that you can leave behind
when you die. It's that powerful.

— JOHN (FIRE) LAME DEER

There wasn't a dry eye in the place as a group of children, ages 2 to 14, sang, "Love is something if you give it away, give it away, you will end up having more."

Many people at Jenny's funeral had learned the song from her at circle time or while she made them lunch or walked them to the park. Today some brought their children and grandchildren to honor her.

Jenny graduated with honors in pediatric nursing. She could have built a powerful career in medicine. She deserved to make more money and have better furniture. But she wanted to heal special needs children one at a time, and she did for fifty years. Today just for her, those children, grown and small, dried their tears and sang her song again, " . . . you will end up having more."

Your gifts of love are so powerful; they will last longer than anything you can imagine.

Childhood is terribly perishable.
It is always under siege.

— JIM GREENMAN

At Mandy's family child care home, Ralph's mother says to her son, "You need to stand up so we can get your coat on." The three year old remains sitting on the floor, so his mom repeats, "You need to stand up."

"But I don't need to; I can do it down here," Ralph replies.

"We can't help you very well unless you stand," his mother says.

"Oh," Ralph says, "You need me to stand up." He scrambles to his feet.

Then his mother says, "Oh, dear, you've got chalk smudges on your face. You need to wipe those off before we leave."

Again Ralph balks, "They don't hurt."

"Let's start over," his mother says. "I need to wipe those smudges from your face." She reaches for her handkerchief.

Ralph submits to the face rubbing, saying, "You need to, because you don't want people to see your boy with a dirty face, huh?"

Mandy says quietly, "Out of the mouths of babes . . ."

In the loving environment you provide, children feel safe to speak out their wisdom as they strive to reason out the demands they meet.

*I have heard their groans and sighs, and seen their
tears, and I would give every drop of blood in my veins
to free them.*

— HARRIET TUBMAN

"Anybody know who Martin Luther King is?"
I ask as I pick up a book about Dr. King from the
reading center. It is the first time I am subbing at
this center.

"He's dead. Some guys shot him," answers five-
year-old Monty from the art table. "They didn't
want black people to be free."

"You know a lot about this, don't you?"

"Yeah, cause some guys shot my brother. He's
dead too." Monty draws slowly with the red marker.

"I'm very sorry."

"Sure."

The assistant teacher takes me aside. "Random
shooting, two years ago. Monty's brother was eight.
He used to come here. Sweet kid."

You hear children tell history through their lives.
You help to free them from their pain when you
listen and understand.

When you get involved, you feel the sense of hope and accomplishment that comes from knowing you are working to make things better.

— PAULINE R. KEZER

The window sign reads, "Licensed Child Care," and out front of the house Jack, an eighteen-year-old college freshman, gets out of his car. Five school-aged kids, seven and eight years old, run to meet him. "You're late," they say.

Watching from the living room window, Jack's mother laughs and tells a visiting friend, "They don't let him get by with being even a few minutes late.

"But the child care idea was his. He wants to work with kids, and some of the neighborhood kids, home alone after school, had formed a little mall gang and were getting into trouble. Their parents had asked me if I could watch them.

"So Jack suggested we get into school-age child care together. And I love it.

"Jack has them doing a neighborhood newsletter; today's delivery day. That's why they're out there waiting for him. They're the neatest kids. They just need to know people care about them," Jack's mother says as a child hurries by and hands her a newsletter. "Hot off the press," the child says proudly.

Because you're involved, you see kids' potential and they feel your hope that the world will value them as you do.

It is better to protest than to accept injustice.

— ROSA PARKS

Alice, a child care provider, is going to appear on TV. She will read an editorial that she wrote urging other providers to go on strike for one day.

"What if somebody from my office sees you stirring up trouble?" her husband asks anxiously.

"People need to understand that parents can't work without us, but most of them can't afford to pay us what we're worth, either. The whole community needs to chip in and take care of its kids."

"Look," her husband says, "We're doing okay."

"Yeah, because you sell machines and make four times what I do."

"There's nothing wrong with what I do."

"I didn't say there was," says Alice, "But raising the next generation is at least as valuable. When the toddler teacher couldn't afford to take her own kids in for strep tests, I knew I had to do something. Come on, show a little support here. My knees are shaking just thinking about those cameras."

It may not be easy, but when you keep working for justice those who care for our children will benefit from your protests. Way to go, shaking knees and all!

Nobody has ever measured, not even poets,
how much the heart can hold.

— ZELDA FITZGERALD

Paul, a first grader, comes to Marie's house after school, except on Thursdays when he attends speech therapy sessions. Last week, Paul's mom told Marie that the Thursday session was canceled. "At home he doesn't stutter or lisp anymore," she said, "but his teacher says it still happens in reading class. Something's strange about this."

On Thursday Paul is downcast about the cancellation so Marie has a chance to explore what is happening. She says, "Paul, I'm sorry you're sad about being here."

"Oh, I'm not sad about that," Paul exclaims. "I'm sad that I won't see Miss Riley."

"But aren't you glad that soon you won't need the speech class?" Marie asks.

"I'll always need it, because I'm never going to read, 'See Spot jump. See Jane run,'" he says, clearly pronouncing each word.

"Because if I say 'Th-th-th-ee Spot th-th-th-ump. Th-th-th-ee Jane run,' I get to go to Miss Riley's class."

Children let you into their hearts because they know you treasure the immeasurable love you find flourishing there.

To be educated meant you could take your place in life.
— Ardie Clark Halyard

After the "big kids" leave for school, the preschoolers gather for stories and songs. "Now I know my ABCs. Next time won't you sing with me," the five kids sing.

"I can say my ABCs," brags Grace.

"Do you want to say them for us?" I ask.

Grace breezes through the letters and ends "W, x, y, z. Did I get them right?"

"You certainly did," I answer.

Looking satisfied, with a small curl of a smile, she says, "Good, now I can get on with my life."

You give children the self-esteem and skills they need to boldly take their places in the world.

Believing in yourself and liking yourself is all
a part of good looks.

— SHIRLEY LORD

The nearby elementary school principal invited Charlene to bring the kids in her care for a photo session.

When the day came, excited four-year-old Rose Marie arrived wearing her ankle-length "Little House on the Prairie" calico dress and favorite straw hat, misshapen from on-and-off tugging.

Today the pictures arrive, and as the kids gather around, Charlene says, "Rose Marie, you're going to love yours." She hands Rose Marie a photo where her straight brown hair frames her face under the uneven brimmed hat, her wire rims perch jauntily on her nose, and she beams a wide, tooth-missing smile.

When her mom comes, Rose Marie waves the photo envelope saying, "You'll want to buy them all. I look so great."

While she skips off to get her carryall, her mom says to Charlene, "You've done so much for her self-esteem through it all—the glasses, the missing teeth, and the hair that won't curl. She's a lucky little girl."

Your skillful guidance through childhood trauma builds fragile self-esteem so even the most vulnerable youngsters see themselves as they are and like what they see.

Imagine the joy of day by day growing into a fuller understanding of who you are—who you are, really, the power you really have.

— Tae Yun Kim

"You should teach some classes," Gail told Clarice. "You know so much about kids."

"I think not," responded Clarice, picking up stray mittens.

That night Clarice attended a workshop on science projects. She surprised herself by filling in her own name on the evaluation sheet where it asked for other possible instructors. "I could teach classes on dealing positively with children," she wrote.

"Nothing will come of it," she thought.

Something did come of it; the coordinator asked her to teach a class. Clarice agreed, mostly out of shock. At the end of her first session, the group filled out the evaluations. Fearfully she read them.

"Great class! Down to earth and extremely helpful."

"I'll never deal with kids the same again."

"Have this instructor back often."

"You bet I'll be back!" Clarice said, doing joyful mental gymnastics all the way home.

You have a wealth of knowledge and deserve to experience the power and joy of sharing it with others.

Try saying "please" and "thank you" and
"do you mind"—this is the language of love.

— JILL BRISCOE

Ten-year-old Dan waits at the Kids' Club door for his mom, hoping his friend Adam can go home with him. As Dan's mom approaches, Adam whispers, "Let me ask her."

"Mrs. Colson," Adam says, "Dan has invited me to your home. Could I please come? Please just say no if it's not convenient."

Dan listens in awe. Bruce, the after-school teacher, raises his eyebrows while Dan's mom says, "You'll have to call your mother."

The boys run to the office phone and back saying, "It's okay."

Dan's mom then asks if Adam likes chicken.

He says, "I'm sure whatever you serve will be delicious."

Dan nudges him sharply and hisses, "Don't overdo your manners."

Adam hisses back, "It works. Manners will get ya everywhere."

The teacher whispers to Adam, helping him with his jacket, "But there is such a thing as overkill."

Good manners are a powerful skill on which social relationships depend; and a loving gift to the kids who learn them from you.

*Let children know your concerns and opinions
and listen to theirs.*

— DR. BENJAMIN SPOCK

Joshua sat in the beanbag chair, chatting with his red dinosaur.

"Are you scared, Red? TV said that there's a war and that kids bring guns to school. Don't worry, I won't let you die."

After listening to Joshua, I decided to start "news time," knowing that children are less fearful when they can feel a sense of empowerment in scary situations. We talked about the news. We wrote a letter to the President telling him to end the war soon. At a toy store, we asked the manager to have more toys that aren't violent.

How proud we were when the President wrote to us and when the toy store sent us rainbow stickers along with a promise to buy good toys!

You know that children are aware of problems much bigger than they are. When you and other adults listen to, comfort, and join with kids, they don't have to feel so scared.

*In moments when you are touched by the soul
of a child . . . you suddenly realize the significance
of these precious years.*

— SHIRLEY DOBSON

Jasmine's Aunt Mae works in a children's hospital where she has gotten close to ten-year-old Stacey, a cystic fibrosis patient. A few months back, Mae had enlisted Jasmine's help in shopping for clothes for Stacey's Barbie doll collection. Today, helping Stacey gather the clothes into a box, Mae suddenly misses her bouncy, energetic niece.

Mae stops to see the six year old on the way home, and Jasmine greets her with a big smile. Tilting her head back, between clenched teeth, Jasmine says, "Notice anything different?"

"You've lost a tooth!" Mae says. "Did the tooth fairy come?"

"Yep. She left a dollar," Jasmine says. "I put my tooth in a plastic bag under my pillow, and she didn't take it."

"Why not, do you suppose?" Mae asks.

"Daddy says she didn't want to disturb me. I think it's because she's going to come again so I'll have two dollars to buy Barbie stuff for Stacey."

Kids learn about caring from you and tuck it away in their souls for when their world needs a touch of childish compassion.

I no longer need my blanket to survive.

— MARIA CAMPBELL

Marcus, 10, works the beach. He wraps himself up in one of his brilliant red, gold, and white blankets and tries to sell the rest to tourists as they sip drinks out of coconuts. Sometimes there isn't enough money for food at his house so he skips school in order to work. His teacher and a group of mothers and grandmothers meet regularly to discuss their children's problems.

"We want them learning so that they can have a better life," Marcus' mom says.

The group writes a hundred letters to store owners about their handwoven blankets and cloth. If enough stores sell their products for a fair price, the children can go to school every day. Two stores agree to try.

"That is a good beginning," the teacher says. "Come to my house Saturday. We will write a hundred more letters. We will keep trying, for the children."

When you join with families to help children, your efforts improve their chances for a bright future.

Be proud of the job you do. Never feel put down
because of it.

— DOROTHY SMITH

Monday, when Esther reached out for one-year-old Devin, who had never been in child care, he clung to his mother and sobbed in Esther's arms after she left. Tuesday, he also cried, holding his arms out to his mom until she closed the door behind her.

Today's Wednesday and when his mother hands Devin to Esther, he leans toward her eagerly.

"I knew he'd love you," his mother says. "I'm so glad you're still in child care."

"Remember when you were five?" Esther asks. "You cried because you had to go to school and wouldn't be coming any more. Your mother took our picture, 'so she'll always remember you,' she said. And you did."

"You're a jewel," Devin's mother says. Smiling, Esther shrugs, "What can I say? I love my work. It's so rewarding."

Take inspiration from Esther's story, full of pride and reasons to value yourself as a caregiver. Feel your worth as you make your way through your day.

When people ask me what qualifies me to be a writer for children, I say I once was a child. But I was not only a child. I was, better still, a weird little kid . . . there are few things, apparently, more helpful to a writer than having once been a weird little kid.

— KATHERINE PATERSON

Charles smiles, chats to himself, and leaves a trail of paper scraps, glitter, and garbage wherever he goes. He doesn't have special friends, although kids play with him sometimes. He is never mean and has some really interesting things to say if anyone listens. One day, Amber, age 5, asked her friend, six-year-old Katlin, what was wrong with Charles.

"Oh," answered Katlin, "he's just weird. You know, like smart people and grown-ups."

You appreciate kids for who they are. Who knows, they may be doing research for being a writer or a child care provider or some other weird, smart, grown-up thing.

You curl your hair and paint your face.
Not I:
I am curled by the wind, painted by the sun.

— JULIA DE BURGOS

As we headed to the sand dune for a picnic, the March wind played with the towels, wrapped around the children's shoulders. I looked at the children, their varying shades of brown skin against the azure shore, and I knew that my small place in this universe is a very important one indeed.

Bringing nature and beauty to children is one of the many gifts you give that will last a lifetime.

Only justice can stop a curse.

— ALICE WALKER

Introducing themselves, most of the twenty-five people in the room say this is their first class in Early Childhood Development.

Risa Hamilton, however, says, "I've always wanted to work with kids. In my teens I was a baby-sitter and since high school I've worked in a child care center. Not much money there, but I also waitress so I can get my degree. Finally, this is my last class."

Everyone applauds and the instructor says, "Risa knows the child care field doesn't pay well, but she's here anyhow. Fortunately for kids, she is one of those wonderful people who is dedicated to them. There's no more important job. But if money, prestige, or even justice in the workplace is what you want, you're looking at the wrong field. We'll talk about the syllabus next week. See you then."

Next week comes, and Risa and fourteen others take their seats. The instructor looks about and says ruefully, "The raw truth always shrinks this class to a manageable size."

Your income should be the envy not the curse of the working world; but until justice prevails, may grateful applause ring in your heart.

Heroism consists in hanging on one minute longer.

— NORWEGIAN PROVERB

I went to bed relieved. "Tomorrow I'm telling Anthony's mother," I thought. "I'll say, 'He scratched yet another child. The parents are upset. You refuse to go to counseling. This is it.'"

In the morning they arrived, cold and tired. "You be a good boy now," Anthony's mother said.

"He surely tries," I said, wrapping him in a quilt and swallowing my well-rehearsed speech.

That night Anthony's mom announced, "I called the counselor today. Something in the love you had this morning made me brave enough. He really does try, doesn't he?"

You are a hero when you hang on for the children who need a second chance to have happy, healthy todays and successful tomorrows.

In crying and in song the children of the world are one.
Let the children of the world say "brother."

— Luchi Blanco de Cuzco

Bob returns from dropping his preschooler at Soo Ling's house and asks his wife, Annette, if she knew about Markie.

"Sure, he's David's best friend from child care. The one he talks about all the time. The one I asked you to pick up today. His mom's car wasn't working, and Soo Ling called and asked if we could do that. I said we would. Didn't you get him?" Annette asks.

"I did. But did you know that he's African American?" Bob asks.

"Well, yes. Why?"

"I was just surprised that David has never mentioned that," Bob says.

"Markie has probably never mentioned that David is Asian American, either," Jane says. "Soo Ling blends a beautiful rainbow. I just love her for that."

You strengthen their generation by teaching kids to value each other, helping them weave their differences into the fabric of one world.

You will do foolish things, but do them with enthusiasm.

— COLETTE

"Look at me, Sadie. Watch the bubbles."
Little drool bubbles dripped down Trace's mouth.

Six-month-old Sadie did the same thing.

"Oh, you're a genius," Trace said, giving her a snuggly hug.

"You are a baby-loving nut aren't you?" asked Sadie's father. Trace had no idea that he had been watching.

Her red face of embarrassment blossomed into a rosy smile as she answered, "Yes, I am, and proud of it too!"

Your loving enthusiasm is the stuff that trust, nurturing, and bonding are made of—don't let anyone tell you it is foolishness.

*You've got to do your own growing, no matter how tall
your grandfather was.*

— IRISH PROVERB

Johnny's dad comes to get him and finds him
whizzing around the gym on a Big Wheel bicycle.
Gregory, the preschool teacher, calls out, "Nate,
your dad's here."

"His name's Johnny," his dad says.

"It is? Oh, that's really funny," Gregory laughs.
"You know what happened? On my first day here,
while trying to get all the kids' names straight,
I said, teasing, 'And you must be Johnny Jump Up.'
He said, 'I'm not Johnny Jump Up. I'm named for
my grandpa.' So I asked, 'What's your grandpa's
name?' He said, 'Grandpa Nate.'"

"In a sense Johnny's right. Nate is his middle
name," Johnny's dad explains.

"I always call him Nate. He's never corrected me."

On the way out, his dad asks Johnny why he lets
the teacher's mistake go on.

"Mommy says I'm going to be tall like grandpa.
Can't get grown-up with a little kid's name. I'm
trying Nate."

**Kids feel secure about testing out their theories about
growing up on you because they can count on your love
and your good humor even when the joke's on you.**

Every adult needs a child to teach. It's the way adults learn.

— Anonymous

Each day at story time, Abbie snuggled up next to me. Sometimes I would give her a little hug. One day I whispered, "I think you just like to be loved."

Looking up at me with her big brown eyes she said, "Doesn't everybody?"

Teachers come in all sizes. Because you lovingly listen to their lessons, children often teach you to be wise.

Just enjoy your ice cream while it's on your plate—that's my philosophy.

— THORNTON WILDER

Several months ago, Nadine left Charlene's house wiping away tears, distressed at having to put six-month-old Joel into child care. As he developed, learning to sit alone and play with his rattles and toys, Charlene recorded his progress and every day gave Nadine what she laughingly called Joel's report card.

Today the "report" said Joel had crawled across the room nonstop. "I'm missing so much of his growing up," Nadine cried, hugging Joel to her.

Charlene asked softly, "What does he do at home?"

"Oh, he's loads of fun," Nadine replied. "He tries to feed himself and makes a real mess. Gets more of it in his hair than his mouth. He looks so funny. And he knows what makes us laugh." Then she stops, smiling.

"Thanks, Charlene," she says. "I get the message. You're so good for him and for me."

You handle your complex job well when you help parents appreciate opportunities they have to enjoy their kids before those chances melt away like ice cream on a dessert plate.

We have made a space to house our spirit, to give form to our dreams.

— JUDY CHICAGO

The art area has an easel, brushes, and jars of paints dripping fuchsia, mahogany, and five other colors. Dominique skips into the sunlit corner. Swirling, thick fingerpaint art, textured collages, and pastel watercolors adorn the walls, forming a small gallery of children's spirits.

Pulling an arm through the backward shirt, Dominique singsongs, "I'm painting a wish today. I'm painting a wish today, today, today."

You make room for children to build dreams for tomorrow and to live lovely todays.

Happiness is like jam. You can't spread even a little without getting some on yourself.

— UNKNOWN

A new family has moved in across the street from Jocelyn's child care home, and every day a little girl sits on the front steps looking quite lonely. Joycelyn suggests that her eight-year-old daughter, Nancy, invite the child over.

"She can't play after school," Nancy announces, matter-of-factly. "She takes care of her little brother. Her name's Leeann."

On Saturday, Joycelyn visits Leeann's mother who explains that she leaves for work when Leeann gets home from school.

"Benny's ten months old. He's napping when I leave, and Leeann needs only to listen in case her brother wakes up," she says. "Their dad gets home about 5:30."

"So I offered to take the kids in the afternoon," Joycelyn later tells her husband.

"Joy, you can't take on the world," he says.

"I'm just taking on a little a girl and her brother for a few hours," Joycelyn replies. "I'm happy; their mom is delighted. And Leeann jumped with joy at the news."

When you lighten the hearts of children, you spread happiness around—a little on you, a lot on them, and everyone they meet.

The decisions we make now affect the seven generations of children to come.

— AMERICAN INDIAN WISDOM,
THROUGH CAROL PEIRCE

Many people at the meeting wanted to sell the land by the lake where the children come every summer. The kids, who have various physical and emotional challenges, come to listen to birds, not guns, and to feel belonging, not ridicule. The kids' parents believe that their children heal in body and spirit when they return to the open arms of nature and the camp counselors. "Our town can use the money for our own," huffed the council chair. "The fire station needs improvements."

Kevin, a local resident and camp volunteer, said, "Mr. Chair, if we need the cash, we could find an alternate site for the kids—maybe the community center. And we could share our homes."

Four council people gasped loudly. The chairperson exhaled his words, "I don't want that riffraff anywhere near my family."

"Probably not, but they're great kids, not riffraff," said Kevin. "Let's do the humane thing now and keep the camp open."

Adults make decisions that generations of children have to live with. You are their voice for truth, fairness, and compassion.

It takes a whole village to raise a child.

— AFRICAN PROVERB

Alan, a kindergartner, gets off the school bus with Dougie, his friend. The substitute driver checks her list and says, "Whoa, Alan. You don't get off yet."

"I don't go to child care anymore. I go to Dougie's house," says Alan.

"That right?" the driver asks. Dougie nods yes.

Meantime, Rachel, the child care mom who takes care of Alan, waits down the road for the bus. When it pulls up and Alan isn't on it, she worriedly asks for him.

The driver explains what happened, and Rachel hurries home with the other three kids she has in tow. She quickly calls a neighbor, who comes over to help with the kids and gets Dougie's home number from telephone information service.

Rachel calls Dougie's mom, who confirms that Alan came home with her son. She assures Rachel he can stay until his dad gets home. Next, she calls Alan's dad at work. Finally, she calls the school principal to alert her to loopholes that clever kids get through.

Your love and concern lead the way in the network of care that makes up the village it takes to raise a child.

Hear me! A single twig breaks, but the bundle of twigs is strong.

— TECUMSEH

"Row, row, row your boat," sang the preschoolers sitting in a cardboard refrigerator box. Jill leaned over and one side of the box ripped open. The kids spilled onto the carpet.

"Get back in and roar, roar, roar your boat," yelled little Corrine.

Children keep going on merrily despite the little "breaks" in their day. As long as they have the strength from you and each other "life is but a dream."

Do you hear the children weeping, O my brothers?
— ELIZABETH BARRETT BROWNING

At 9 a.m., the phone and doorbell ring simultaneously at Morgan Keith's house. She opens the door and motions five-year-old Kristin to come in.

Kristin's mom is on the phone saying, "The school called. Kristin didn't get on the bus. She said she was going to Mrs. Keith's and ran down the street. Is she there?"

While they wait for her mom to come, Kristin, who's in Morgan's after-school home care, pours out her story.

"My daddy's going to die. He was really crabby this morning because I spilled my milk," she sobs.

Morgan holds Kristin until her mom arrives. Her mom says, "When my father visited last week, he was impatient with Kristin. I explained grandpa wasn't well, not his usual self. He died the next day. We've all been having a bad time.

"John yelled at Kristin this morning, and I had no idea what she was thinking. She was scared and ran to you."

Kids know you will hear them and understand when they weep.

. . . we can only understand when we start talking to each other. And this is the only way to correct our ideas.

— RIGOBERTA MENCHU

I read a book about families who work in avocado fields like the ones outside our room. One curious four year old ran to the window and asked, "Do they sleep out there at night?"

"We can find out," I answered.

The next week a migrant worker and her little girl visited us. They told us where they sleep, that the drinking water is dirty, and the kids have no toys.

"That would make my mom mad!" said Georgia.

Actually, Georgia's mom was angry that I taught things that "little ones can't understand." Other parents, motivated by their kids' concerns, organized a friendship club with the migrant families. Georgia's mom put her in a different program where "they teach the important things."

You teach children to look out the window and listen to each others' stories. You can be proud of the difference your efforts make in people's lives.

If they drop a slice of bread on the carpet, it will inevitably land buttered side down!

— SHIRLEY DOBSON

Six-year-old Gary has the day off from school. He'll spend it with Ursula, who does home care. He runs up the walk, trips on his untied shoelaces, and spills his board game. His dad gets out of the car and picks up game pieces, all the while chastising Gary, "Why aren't your shoes tied? Do it now!"

Gary pulls off his gloves. He gets the shoes somewhat tied, but leaves his gloves in his hurry to catch up with his dad.

"Where are your gloves?" his dad asks. Gary runs back for them. He trips, falls, scrambles to his feet. Ursula waits at the door.

"The kid's such a clutz!" says his dad.

Ursula ushers Gary in. "We all make mistakes, don't we?" she says.

Gary's dad pauses, says, "I sure do," and gives Gary a bear hug. Patting him on the seat of his jeans, he tells Gary, "You're just normal, kid—like the rest of us."

You realize how much "clutzy" kids need assurance that they're all right—it's the world that's impatient.

. . . you will never put me in a corner anywhere.
I would build myself a round room first so that there
would be no corners.

— JUANITA JEWEL CRAFT

Beverly was angry enough not to be afraid to meet with the director, Louise.

"You want to talk to me?" asked Louise.

"Yes," began Beverly. "I've never been comfortable with how rigid things are here. Everybody has to have the same schedules and themes. We have to line up kids too often. I can't be creative at all. I've tried to adjust because I'm pretty new. But today, when you made two-year-old Casey sit in a corner for fifteen minutes for crying, that was the end."

"When you've been at this as long as I have, hon, you'll know there have to be rules," Louise said, patting Beverly's arm.

"Not rules that stifle people's spirits. I have to quit," Beverly said, feeling a rush of lightness in her heart that she had almost forgotten.

When you build a world for children of respect, exploration, and love, their spirits will never be pushed into a corner.

The universe is made of stories, not of atoms.

— MURIEL RUKEYSER

When the doorbell rings, Laurie glances at her watch and wonders aloud, "Who could that be so late?"

She switches on the outdoor light and looks out at Keith, Mary Beth's father.

The two year old hadn't been coming to Laurie's this week because she was sick, running a high fever. A stab of fear hits Laurie as she opens the door.

"Is something wrong?" she asks.

"No, No," Keith says. "Mary Beth's much better. I really feel foolish asking this, but could we borrow the record, 'Hurrah, Hurrah! Today's My Birthday!'? Sorry about the time. I know it's past nine, but we can't get her to settle down. She says she will if we play that record for her."

"Come in, come in," Laurie says. "A picture book goes with it. I'll get it for you."

The songs and stories you share with families gives them insight into the world of learning and growing that their children share with you.

I am convinced that we must train not only the head,
but the heart and hand as well.

— MADAME CHIANG KAI-SHEK

It took an hour of careful nailing and gluing to make her wooden creation.

"It's a wishing tree," Emily proudly explained to her mother. "You talk to it and things come true."

"Don't get slivers from that thing," her mother said. "Did you learn any letters today?"

By training their hearts and hands, you allow children to learn new skills, imagine incredible things, and make wishes that could come true.

A child should not be denied a balloon because an adult knows it will burst.

— MARCELENE COX

Kids romp in the gym but six-year-old Manuel sits in a corner with a book. Jose, a teacher in the after-school program, approaches. "Manuel," he asks, "What are you reading?" Manuel hands him his large picture book and another slender book falls from it.

Jose picks up the smaller book. "You can read this?" he asks.

"Si," Manuel says eagerly and recites, "I wandered lonely as a cloud that floats on high o'er vales and hills, when all at once I saw a crowd, a host, of golden daffodils . . ."

"Wonderful! That's William Wordsworth," Jose interrupts.

Manuel replies, "My mother says someday I can write such a book. Papa says it is wrong; I should study what will earn money."

"No need to hide it here, Manuel. When we have our spring program, you can read from that book. Your papa will be proud. You will see," Jose says, leaving the boy with the poetry book on his knee and the picture book on the floor.

You let kids dream the dreams of which visions are made that could burst like balloons without your encouragement and support.

If you love somebody enough, you can still hear the laughter after they're gone.

— AL BAKER

"Lights, camera, action!" Jesse proclaimed before his first big vacation. Through his thick-lensed glasses he constantly took pictures. Susie, his caregiver, gave him a camera for the trip.

"What kind of a gift is that for a kid who can hardly see?" one of the other kids asked.

Jesse let the unkind words slink into the place where hundreds of such remarks hide, and said, "Thanks."

"When you get back, I shall see what you saw," Susie laughed.

At a silky beach Jesse coaxed sand together into a mound. He held seashells close to his eyes, examining the delicate patterns. He placed the prettiest ones on the mound.

His dad wanted to move on, but Jesse waited for the light to be just right for a picture. "Now Susie can see that I saw seashells at the seashore," he said with a laugh that sounded a little like an echo.

Your sensitive care and loving laughter will follow children as they go off on their own to see the world.

You cannot shake hands with a clenched fist.

— Indira Gandhi

Darryl, three years old, and Kay, his five-year-old sister, live in Judy and Joe Gleeson's foster home. Their mom has a history of finding reliable care for Kay but leaving Darryl with abusive sitters and confining him to a crib.

As a result, Darryl is developmentally delayed and says few words. People who cared for him struck him, so he hits at those he likes.

After several months, Darryl continues to show affection with his fists and the Gleesons still have to keep doors locked so he doesn't bolt wildly out. Judy felt discouraged and ready to give up until today. Joe, returning Kay from school, turned the key in the lock and opened the door, prepared to ward off Darryl's pummeling greeting.

Judy automatically reached her arm out to restrain Darryl. But he encircled himself into it, pressed against her, and said, "Love you."

"Oh," Judy gasped, "You do get it! I love you too."

Those who have known only violence, have only violence to give. When you teach kids gentleness, you give a legacy of love to their world.

It is the obligation of all human beings to do what is right for children.

— BEV BOS

One afternoon a month, I attend meetings of a statewide task force designed to improve children's well-being. I have to find a sub, explain to parents why I'll be gone, and take three buses to get there. I am the only child care provider. The other members come from business and government. At the last meeting, I suggested that the business community should explore ways to help fund child care.

"You've taken mothers into the workforce, usually at low wages. Now you need to pay to replace them," I said. "Child care workers' salaries are lower than those of animal keepers."

The chairman of a huge corporation said, "Look, dear, we're not interested in baby-sitting. We must educate our future workers."

"That's what I do," I answered. "I educate children to be caring, competent, human beings."

You do what is right for children when you speak out. Your thoughtful, powerful words educate others to understand that we all must care for the children.

If indeed you must be candid, be candid beautifully.

— KAHLIL GIBRAN

Karen, the county licenser, waits for Ruth Brown to answer the door. Ruth has been nervously anticipating this visit since she applied for a home care license.

Hers is an older home. It's fall and a mouse, looking for winter warmth, has found its way in. Ruth set a trap near the refrigerator a few days ago where the critter left telltale signs. On her way to the front door, she hears the trap snap and says, "Oh, no. Not now." Snatching it up, she hurries into the bathroom.

There, she releases the trap into the toilet, and flushes. The mouse briefly appears to swim. Lourd, her three-year-old son, watches but says nothing until she opens the door for Karen. Then he shouts, "Quick, Mommy, come see. The mousie's still wimmin' in the toilet."

You free kids to be beautifully candid because you can find humor in their childish openness.

*Life deals us a set of cards and then says, "Here, see
what you can do with them." To take an unbalanced or
mediocre hand and play it brilliantly—this is what
makes the game exciting.*

— DOROTHY HOPPER

Janet says to the children, "You need to work
together here, cooperate. Be proud and say I'm glad
I'm an African-American."

The group is practicing to sing at a conference.
Janet leads them with all her heart. She knows
what it's like to be called names and be spat upon,
but she finished school anyway. She knows what
it's like to be poor, raise five kids alone, get them
through being called names and shot at, and make
sure they all finish college too. She's done it all and
more. The little kids she works with trust her. They
put their chests out and their heads up and sing
together in a loud strong voice.

**By watching you play your hand brilliantly, children
learn that they can be proud of who they are.
You give them the inspiration to take what life
deals them and come out winners.**

We must do the things we think we cannot do.

— ELEANOR ROOSEVELT

The staff meeting's discussion is about Janine, a seven year old who has been in the after-school program for three weeks.

"She takes so much time," a teacher argues.

"It's exasperating," another staff member says. "If the line goes left, she goes right. If we tell her it's okay not to do something that's difficult for her, she screams and throws things."

"Look, we know Janine has severe dyslexia and other problems," the director says. "But she's bright. She just gets angry and frustrated because learning is a struggle and she's tired when she gets here. Four other centers have said they couldn't work with her. She's had enough rejection and we can help her. Let's just do it."

Some staff grumble, but they shrug their shoulders, scoop their chairs closer to the table, and go to work for a child who needs them.

Start your day feeling proud for all the times you've gone beyond what you thought you could not do, and helped kids overcome their challenges.

Those who know how to play can easily leap over the adversities of life. And one who knows how to sing and laugh never brews mischief.

— IGLULIK PROVERB

Farah was a new mom. Nervously, she started looking for care for her daughter, Erin. She got a list of places that met the basic standards.

"I'll know it when I see it," she told herself.

At her fourth stop, she interrupted a person who was up to her elbows in soggy soil and was singing. Farah assumed she was a gardener. "Excuse me," she said. "Could you tell me where to find the child care center?"

"I sure can," laughed the mud-caked woman. "Hi! I'm the director. I was just getting the afternoon mud-making activities organized. I think you'll like us. Kids sure do!"

You join children as they play and sing. You teach them to live with laughter, leap for joy, and love the squishy earth. And they like you for it, they sure do!

Success is never a destiny—it's a journey.

— Satenig St. Marie

When the Mother's Club recruited their kids to entertain at a benefit fundraiser, Warren, a first grader, said, "I can't sing or dance and do stuff."

But his mom urged him to think about it. "Maybe you could help Marianna and Louis," she said. "They're preschoolers, but their mother says Marianna dances a little. And Louis wants to do something."

On Tuesday, Warren excitedly announced, "My teacher gave me an idea, but I have to check it out with grandpa."

Today is Sunday and "Act V: Marianna, Louis, and Warren with Mike" is onstage. Marianna in pink tights and tutu twirls charmingly, followed by Mike, a medium-sized, gray-white-black shaggy dog also sporting a pink tutu, spinning around on his hind legs. Alongside, Louis keeps him dancing with bits of food.

Marianna and Louis exit while Warren tells Mike, his grandpa's dog, to "Thank the audience," now on their feet applauding. The dog goes into his finale— dancing, rolling over, playing dead—ending with a paws-crossed, head-down, rump-in-the-air, deep bow.

Take a bow for teaching kids to find success in the small triumphs they'll meet in life's journey ahead.

Life is what I make it, always has been, always will be.
— GRANDMA MOSES

Tearfully thanking everyone, I retired after teaching preschool for thirty-five years. I was sad but secretly I looked forward to no more runny noses, worried parents, or skimpy budgets. After a year, however, I realized that the hole I felt each day could only be filled by children. I volunteered at a nursery school. I sang, made playdough, and felt full of life again. Jamar, an eager, gifted four year old, often came to me to solve problems like how to count sand. One day, after I helped him figure out why the sky is blue, he said, quite seriously, "You really should think about being a teacher."

Children admire the gifts that you share with them. You make their lives and yours full of joy, discovery, and respect.

There's so much to learn when one's only just ten.

— MARGARET JOHNSON

A reporter and photographer from City News are doing a piece on an inner city preteen "Kids at Work" after-school program.

They go into the workroom where they interview LaTavia, 12, who's replacing a broken spring on a toy truck for the upcoming community toy drive. They next visit the computer room where Riza and Kevin are working on the center's newsletter.

"If you want a graphic on the page, transport in something from clip art," ten-year-old Riza's telling Kevin.

"And how come you haven't got a page design?" she asks.

Kevin bristles, "Hey, I'm just learning this stuff. I'm only eleven."

Mia, the project supervisor, steps in. "What's the trouble?" she asks.

The reporter whispers to the photographer, "How old do you suppose she is?"

"Probably all of twelve," replies the photographer.

Mia overhears, looks away from Riza and Kevin, and whispers, "Ten."

Children will always remember you for recognizing their potential and guiding their growing years.

We who have rocked the cradle are now using our heads to rock the boat.

— WILMA SCOTT HEIDE

A group of about forty parents of kids from the child care center meet at Kylie's home over a potluck dinner. The issue is teacher turnover at the center.

"My Katie loves Shannon," Kylie tells the gathering. "After a year and a half, she's leaving. I'm upset about Shannon. But I'm also upset because before her it was Sarah, Peter, Carleen, and on and on.

"They've all tried to hang in, but you know with few if any benefits and such low pay who can expect them to? Every time a teacher or a loved aide leaves, the kids grieve. That's so hard for kids.

"I found out about this Parents For Kids group," she continues, handing out a flyer and a brochure. "As they say, there's strength in numbers, and that's what we need, enough clout to rock the boat."

Just as you deserve the love of a child's hug, you deserve hands willing to rock the boat of injustice for you. Reach out for both and feel their power.

Surround of rainbows
Listen
The rain comes upon us
Restore us.

— MERIDEL LE SUEUR

We visited Sherell at the hospital. It's only three blocks from the apartments where the kids live and have child care so we walked despite the intermittent raindrops. Because we had prepared for our visit, the four year olds expected the green-tiled walls, medicine smells, and sick people. Still, they felt better in the playroom, which had stuffed toys and cartoon murals on the walls.

Sherell sat in a rocker. "You can see our houses from this window," he said.

The kids knew that he had lost his hair because of the medicine, but they didn't care. They were just happy to see their buddy.

"Sherell can come back to our class soon," I said.

Marshall interrupted, "Look out the window!"

A brilliant rainbow arched from the playroom to the apartments. The children oohed and ahhed.

Marshall put his arm around Sherell's shoulder. "See, Sherell," he said wisely, "it's a rainbow bridge to show you the way home."

You build children's strength when you teach them how to deal with life's real problems and yet let them believe in rainbows.

Quite often good things have hurtful consequences.

— ARISTOTLE

Cissie, on break from college, takes the kids in her mom's care for a walk. Two-year-old Edie steps into mud along the sidewalk.

Back home, Cissie wipes off Edie's shoes, but her mom says, "I'm sure her mother would appreciate it if you polished them."

So Cissie washes the laces and polishes the white high tops. When Edie's dad comes, Edie says, "See pretty shoes." Dad thanks Cissie and says, "They look very nice."

Each day after that, Edie arrives wearing freshly polished shoes. On Friday Edie's dad apologizes. "Sorry we didn't get to the shoes," he says. "My wife was so embarrassed that you had to clean them that it has become a daily ritual. It's the old guilt thing with working moms."

Cissie's mom explains about the mud and says, "Cleaning the shoes was to help, not hurt. I'll call Diane. In the meantime," she adds, "Edie, give mommy this for me," and hugs the little girl who giggles and hugs her back.

Your professionalism shows as you heal hurtful misunderstandings and maintain good relationships important to the lives of kids.

When nothing is sure, everything is possible.

— MARGARET DRABBLE

Zoe balances one more little wooden block on top of her tall structure.

"It's gonna fall. It's gonna fall," her four-year-old friend says with fear and a whisper of hope.

"Oh, I think Zoe knows what she's doing," I say, trying to reassure Zoe.

"Ohhhhh, I don't know about that!" Zoe laughs.

"Well, you're good under pressure, then. That's a talent."

Zoe carefully places another block on her somewhat shaky tower.

"What's pressure?" she asks.

When you help kids build confidence, you learn from them—time and again—the importance of letting fear go and letting possibility in.

You may be disappointed if you fail, but you are doomed if you don't try.

— BEVERLY SILLS

In the sun and soft breeze of spring, Tanya, Cheryl, and their group of toddlers walk to the park, bubbles and a kite in tow. The teachers fly the kite for the fascinated kids. After awhile, Tanya says, "Let's do bubbles." But the kids want to stay with the kite. Cheryl passes the kite to a three year old.

"Look, she's doing great," Cheryl shouts to Tanya. All the kids want to try, but Tanya says nervously, "We may have a lot of tears when they can't fly the thing." One after another, however, the children try, beaming and strutting, running to keep the kite aloft, and handing off to each other.

"Look at 'em," Tanya says. "What a challenge! And they literally ran with it."

"Lifts your spirits, huh?" Cheryl laughs, "Like higher than a kite?"

Because you let them try, you give kids faith in themselves, replacing the fear of failure with the courage to risk disappointment and try again.

It is not differences in themselves that cause the problems but how people respond to differences.

— LOUISE DERMAN-SPARKS

Giles, the center director, hands Roderick's mother a plastic bag with three sets of wet clothes. "His teacher had to leave early today, so I'm helping out," Giles explains. "Sorry to give you all of this washing."

"I don't understand," Roderick's mother says. "He is doing well at potty training at home. Why is he having so many accidents here? Does he say, 'Quiero ir al baño'?"

"I don't know," answers Giles. "Why don't I discuss it with the teacher tomorrow and have her get back to you?"

"Gracias, that would be great."

Later, when Giles asks the teacher about Roderick, she replies, "I won't let him go to the bathroom until he speaks in English. He needs to learn to communicate."

"Oh, I think that Roderick is communicating," Giles says, "We need to understand. Let's both talk to his mom tonight and see if we can learn a thing or two."

Because you take the time to recognize and respond respectfully to differences, the children in your care learn to value themselves and their families.

We all live with the objective of being happy; our lives are all different and yet the same.

— ANNE FRANK

Maggie is the subject of a custody fight between her dad, who is wealthy and remarried, and her mom, who worries that courts will rule against her because she works.

"She'll be here from 3 until 5:30," Maggie's mom tells Doris, a home care provider. "Just keep her safe and happy."

Maggie makes friends in the neighborhood, learns to ride a bike, and becomes a delighted eleven-year-old. Because she is always ready to get into the car, her mom doesn't come to the door. All's well until the first day Maggie doesn't use training wheels; she tips the bike and scrapes her knee.

"What happened?" Maggie's mother shrieks at the sight of the bandage.

Doris hurries from the house to help Maggie explain.

"What was she doing on a bike?" Maggie's mom demands to know, while Maggie pleads, "Let's go, Mommy."

Glaring at Doris, Maggie's mom says, "I told you to keep her safe and happy."

Happiness is an objective that is beyond the reach of children without people like you who know that a carefree slice of childhood is worth the risk of a bandage.

Children must be sheltered by the wing of a caring adult from the discrimination, bias, and ethnocentrism that attempt to uproot them.

— STACEY YORK

Phan, a Hmong-American child care provider, reads books to kids about their Hmong culture. She calls these books "home" books and lets one child a day take a book to share with their family. One day after Phan read the children a picture book, four-year-old Kinh looked up from her space in the circle and said, "I think the people in your books are sooo beautiful."

Your work honors the culture of each child. You provide a caring shelter for children as they learn about themselves and others.

The purpose of play is to go out and be happy . . . to lay down cares and have fun for a while.

— WILLIAM DORN

Angelina and Lela, both 11, Luther, 10, and Mario, 9, take turns as umpire, pitcher, batter, base runners, and coach of imaginary players that make up their teams. Their game is in one corner of the playground, away from the younger kids.

For a while Luther coaches, shouting, "Move to third!" Next, he chats it up at first base, while Mario is at bat. Lela, player and umpire, yells, "You're out!" when she tags Mario at home plate. Loud cheers greet her grand slam as she ties the score four to four.

Beyond the high-wire fence, substandard housing, violence, and other problems wait for them. But for now, they play ball.

You give kids a lifelong survival skill when you teach them how to have fun and banish their worries with play.

When we give unconditional love to children, we give the most valuable gift we have.

— KATHERINE M. OLSON

Trent's mother died. She died at home, hooked up to tubes and holding her son's hand. His father didn't know how to shield Trent from the pain and couldn't deal with the scars it left, so he yelled or was silent.

Trent carried a wild look in his eyes and raging loneliness in his heart. One day when he built a block structure, I said, "Great building."

With a swift kick, he toppled the tower, shouting at me, "Go away, stupid."

"Trent," I said gently, "I am here for you no matter what."

"Not if I call you bad names," he said.

"I don't want you to do that, but I will still love you."

"Not if I spit at you."

"I'll still love you."

He made up more gruesome possibilities. I kept reassuring him.

Finally he asked, "Can I go now?"

"Are you okay to play safely?" I asked.

"Yeah," he answered and tore out.

A second later, he popped back. "I believe you," he said and darted away again.

You give children the most valuable gift when you stand by them even in the toughest of times.

If children are not taken care of, whatever else we do won't matter much.

— HILLARY RODHAM CLINTON

"Come in, Joshua. We'll put your things in the bedroom," Freida says. From the kitchen, Freida's daughter, Ava, calls out, "Mom, you haven't brought one of the kids home!"

"I've brought a guest," Freida replies.

Catching the warning tone, Ava says, "Hello, Joshua. You two are just in time to eat."

Later, with Joshua asleep, Ava says, "Mom, you say you're going to leave child care before the low pay and lack of appreciation make a bitter woman of you. So why do we have a five year old in the spare room?"

"Because his mom has a chance to work this weekend but nowhere to leave him."

"What about your weekend—your craft fair— your big chance to show your work?" Ava asks.

"I'll take him. I'd rather have him by the hand than on my conscience," Freida answers.

"I give up," Ava says. "You may have him by the hand, but he's got you by the heart."

Your commitment to children gives them hope for a just world where they will matter and grow up feeling loved and cherished.

Many things we need can wait, the child cannot . . .
To them we cannot say tomorrow, their name is today.

— GABRIELLA MARELLA

Maria is busy filling out the stack of forms for the state licenser.

Emmanual rests his chin on the table edge. "Remember, Maria? You said we could go to the park."

"I need to get some things done," she replies. "Tomorrow, Emmanual, tomorrow."

He turns slowly. Walking away he says sadly, "Tomorrow never comes."

You do your best work for children each day because their needs cannot wait for some unknown tomorrow.

Little girls are cute and small only to adults. To one another they are not cute. They are life-sized.

— MARGARET ATWOOD

In the housekeeping corner today, the after-school first graders play beauty shop with preschoolers as customers. Megan works on Cinda's short straight bob, pretending to curl it with the handle of a doll-sized hair brush.

Occasionally she stands back to admire her work. Finally she gives Cinda a small mirror and asks, "How is that?"

"It looks very nice," says three-year-old Cinda.

Handing her a toy phone, Megan says, "I'm glad you like it. You can use this phone to call your husband to pick you up." Cinda dials, waits a moment, and then says, "You can come get me now. I have so much curls."

Nearby, a parent visiting with a teacher chuckles. Cinda, sitting with legs crossed and holding the phone in the most sophisticated manner a three year old can muster, says indignantly, "Don't laugh to me."

"Sorry, Cinda," the teacher says. "We didn't mean to eavesdrop."

Your sensitivity makes children unafraid to communicate their "life-sized" feelings as they mirror their world in play.

In search of my mother's garden, I found my own.

— ALICE WALKER

Matted and mangy, the barn cats came out to sun themselves as the snow water dripped off the roof. I sat on the stoop, watching the kids get their shoes muddy and their souls warmed.

I felt grateful for the love that came from somewhere and allowed me to enjoy these kids. My mother would have yelled at them for getting their clothes dirty.

The spring breeze played with the branches of the trees that she had planted when I was little. I remember digging in the dirt with her. She showed me how and then scolded me because I didn't do it just right.

A cat meowed. As I stroked it, I listened to the wind and the children's chatter and thanked my mom for teaching me how to do things. Then I thanked myself for continuing to grow.

You bring the best from your childhood and nurture it and give it to the children in your care so that they can plant their own gardens.

Find something you are passionate about and keep tremendously interested in it.

— JULIA CHILD

Rachel, a toddler teacher on her break, hangs up the phone and says, "What a downer!"

"Problem?" her colleague Vida asks.

"That was a friend," says Rachel. "I said I couldn't go to the health club tonight because I have a child development class. She asked me if I really want to be a glorified baby-sitter all my life. Can you believe that?"

"Oh, sure," Vida says. "My dad asks me when I'm going to get a real job. To top that, last week a woman at a party asked what I did and I said I'm a teacher. Then she asked, 'What grade?' When I said, 'Toddlers,' she said, 'What do you teach them!?'"

"But, hey! Let's look at the upside," Vida says. "One of these kids may be president some day. That'd show 'em!"

Your interest in kids fires the passion for your work where children learn the fundamental values of love and caring on which the tomorrows of society depend.

She left no little things behind
Except loving thoughts and kind.

— ROSE HENNIKER HEATON

"Hi, Connie. I hope I didn't interrupt your dinner."

"Don't I wish," says the somewhat overwhelmed mother of ten-month-old Cory and two-year-old Joy. "I haven't even started making it yet."

"I found Joy's teddy bear wrapped up in Cory's security blanket on the front steps after you left," I say. "I thought you might miss them at bedtime. I'm on my way to a class tonight. I could drop them off on the way."

"Once again you've saved my life," she replies. "Thanks. What would I do without you?"

Maybe tonight a parent will have the time and energy to give a child an extra hug because your thoughts and kindness left no little thing undone.

How dear to my heart are the scenes of my childhood . . .
— SAMUEL WOODWORTH

The center's short of help today so Lois, the director, has squeezed lunch duty into a busy schedule. Lois urges Monty to eat some salad before his pizza and banana, while she opens a milk carton for his friend Antoine.

Then she hurries along to help three-year-old Tyheisha, who, having never seen a hard-boiled egg before, is trying to eat one without removing the shell. Tyheisha giggles at her mistake, and Lois, leaving her with a hug, returns to Monty. Antoine says, "He ate his salad."

"Yeah," Monty says. "So will you peel my banana, please?" He nudges Antoine as Lois hurriedly reaches for the banana. When it collapses at her touch, the boys hoot with laughter. They are delighted at Monty's success in making the peel appear untouched.

Lois feigns complete surprise and says, "Very funny, you two!" She knows she has made their day.

Because you allow occasional mischievous moments to succeed, you etch happy childhood scenes on the hearts of kids, along with a lesson in patience that says "love."

There is always one true inner voice. Trust it.

— GLORIA STEINEM

Curled up under puffy comforters, the two year olds listened to a naptime story about the little engine that overcame great difficulties. I was never sure how many of the words they understood, but I knew just hearing the words was important. After the story, Trent wiggled and giggled on his cot. Afraid he would disturb the other children, I rubbed his back and said, "Try to relax and get some rest time."

He snuggled his head into his pillow, closed his eyes real tight, and whispered, "I think I can. I think I can."

As I felt his little body take deep, sleepy breaths, I hummed, "You knew you could. You knew you could."

Trust that your loving care teaches children to believe in themselves.

We don't know who we are until we see what we can do.
— MARTHA GRIMES

Loretta, an empty-nester missing her grown kids, applied for a child care license. Her licensing interview and the home visit went well, and she soon had four toddlers to care for.

Her friends, feeling freed from child rearing, questioned why she would ever want to do child care, and were baffled that she felt she needed the training classes she enrolled in.

"You could probably teach those classes," they'd say.

Their attitude raised some uncertainty in Loretta, but it vanished the day a neighbor ran to Loretta's house carrying her gasping, choking two-year-old grandson and crying, "Please help me!"

Loretta grasped little Kenny, applied the Heimlich maneuver she had just learned that week, and he coughed out a bite of roll that had lodged in his throat.

Loretta hugged the child close, then gave him to his grandmother and, with a sure step, returned to doing the lunch dishes.

Your love for children defines who you are: a person with a generous heart, giving the best of yourself to kids who need you.

Surely the earth can be saved by all the people who insist on love.

— ALICE WALKER

Faces framed in candlelight float up the road. Voices sing about love and caring. Between songs, the marchers for children's rights tell each other who they are: builders, teachers, parents, students, bankers, doctors, plumbers, social workers, clerks, managers, construction workers.

They whisper to each other, "I am here because I carry children in my heart. I don't talk about it much, but a part of me cries when I hear a suffering child cry. So I am here tonight to learn why they cry and to pledge my time and money to change things."

The voices fade and the candles dim. My dream merges with the morning light and I begin my day.

You insist on love for children. It is your insistence that saves children's dreams and helps them come true.

No one has yet fully realized the wealth of sympathy,
kindness, and generosity hidden in the soul of a child.

— EMMA GOLDMAN

Three-year-old Jordan lies on his cot, pointing toward the ceiling and talking quietly. The toddler teacher approaches and asks why he isn't napping.

"First I have to talk to my grandpa in heaven," Jordan replies. "I don't know how he got way up there. I think maybe on an escalator.

"Anyway, I have to tell him to look down and see my baby sister, Ann, because my mom is sad that he went away before he could see her. I told Mommy he'd open up heaven and see Ann. I'm just reminding him to do that."

Kids open their hearts to you because you empathize with the feelings they hold within them.

We are the curators of life on earth. We hold it in the palm of our hand.

— HELEN CALDICOTT

"Catch, here it comes," Caryl says as she rolls the soft ball with the world printed on it to twenty-month-old Margo. "Nice one. Now push it back to me."

Margo sweeps at the ball and sends it plopping across the floor. Her whole body follows and she bumps her head on the floor.

Caryl drops the earth ball and picks up Margo. "It'll be okay. It'll be okay," she reassures the crying child.

Pointing to the floor, Margo sobs, "Ball, owie. Ball, owie."

Caryl scoops up the ball, kisses it, and then kisses Margo. Margo snuggles her fuzzy head into Caryl's shoulder and coos.

"Now I do have the whole world in my hands, don't I, wonderful one?" Caryl sings.

You are the caretaker of the earth's most wonderful resource: the children. Your tender care allows them to trust that you will make the world a better place.

*Keep your face to the sunshine and you cannot
see the shadows.*

— HELEN KELLER

Rachel, a preschool teacher, arrives with Rinny,
her seeing eye dog. She puts down her guitar case
and greets the children who run to meet her.

"I'm so glad to see you," she says, running her
long, slim fingers over their upturned faces. After
their music session, Benjamin comes to her and
says, "Look at the picture I made for you."

"Tell me about it and the colors you used,"
Rachel says.

"No," Benjamin says, thrusting the paper toward
her. "I want you to really look at it. Feel it."

As Rachel moves her fingers over the drawing,
Benjamin watches and says, "The sun's yellow and
smiling at you and Rinny. That's the grass—all
green. The sky's blue. No clouds, though. I didn't
want shadows."

Putting his hand on Rachel's hand, he asks,
"Now, aren't you glad you really looked at it?"

**You enrich children's lives when you teach them
about people who bravely reach beyond shadows to
the love that awaits them there.**

It is more blessed to give than to receive, so give to yourself as much as you can—as often as you can.

— LA VERNE PORTER WHEATLY PERRY

You deserve a gift today. On a small piece of paper, write down the most fantastic thing about you. You don't have to be shy or humble.

Done? Good.

Now write down why the kids you care for are lucky to have you in their lives.

Great!

Place that piece of paper on the page for May 23—one month from now. When you open the book that day, remember to do something nice for the important, wonderful person you are.

Level with your child by being honest. Nobody spots a phony quicker than a child.

— MARY MACCRACKEN

The fifth-grade teacher asks Bernadette, 11, to read a sentence from the board. When Bernadette can't, the teacher notifies the school nurse.

Bernadette's dad then takes his daughter to the eye doctor who confirms that Bernadette needs glasses. She hates the glasses and stuffs them into her pocket when school is out. The after-school program teacher doesn't know Bernadette has glasses until Bernadette's dad picks her up and discovers the broken glasses in Bernadette's pocket.

The next day, Bernadette, with glasses on, comes to school with her mom.

"Don't you think she looks beautiful with glasses?" Her mom says to Bernadette's teacher. "I've told her over and over that I've never seen a child who could wear them so well. Have you?"

Bernadette bursts into tears. "Mom, will you stop?" she cries. "I look like a geek. And you know it."

You help kids cope because you understand their need for honesty and their ability to deal with it.

The most effective way to do it, is to do it.

— TONI CADE BAMBARA

"She won't let us."

"She might. You ask."

"No, you ask."

"Ask me what?" I inquire of the five-year-old bunch.

Eddie's green eyes flash as the other kids nudge him.

"Wewanttoskipnapwiththelittlekidsandmake cookieswithyou," he says as fast as he can before he loses his nerve.

"Sounds like a plan to me!" I answer.

I leave the room and hear them say, "Told you she would."

"Did not."

"Did too."

Because of your flexibility and understanding, kids take risks, and learn to be direct, respectful, and effective. Greatlessonsforlife!

Take time to laugh—it is the music of the soul.

— ANONYMOUS

Two-year-old Crissie likes everything about coming to Evelyn's while her mom works. She likes the other kids, the toys, the stories, and especially lunch. Her favorite meal is tomato soup with animal crackers and grilled peanut butter sandwiches, which Evelyn served yesterday.

On that day, Crissie sat swinging her feet contentedly and, between spoonfuls and bites, hummed softly, "Ummm good." When the nearby church bell rang at noon, she said in the same humming tone, "Here comes the train."

"That's not a train," the other kids scoffed. "That's the church bell."

Today, when the bell rang, Crissie innocently sang out, "Here comes the church!" The kids laughed and applauded.

"That's a good one, Crissie," they said, and she loved her moment in the limelight.

The time you take to laugh with kids creates good moments to remember, like unforgettable melodies that lift your soul.

In your lifetime if you can come up with one original idea, you have accomplished a lot.

— MAX ROACH

"Okay, I've got it, this one is going to make us millions," I said excitedly.

"Now what?" groaned three other child care workers.

"I know how we're going to raise money for the new playground."

"All right, spit it out. I hope it's a good one this time. Better than the 'Lunch with the Director' raffle," chided one skeptical coworker. "That brought in a whopping $12.62."

"I'm going to write a book called 300 Fund-Raising Ideas You Don't Have to Bother Trying. We Tried Them All and We're Still Broke. Should be a best seller, don't you think?"

You keep scheming, dreaming, and laughing. You are truly an original!

Perhaps the chief business of life is simply to learn how to love.

— MARSHA SINETAR

Faye is six years old and a first grader. She comes to Katherine's family care home before and after school. The court has just recently returned her to her mother who frequently left her alone without supervision. Katherine works with the county worker in reestablishing the family.

Today Faye has an afternoon free because of teacher meetings. As she helps with lunch dishes, she says, "Mom's date last night told me . . . ," and stops. "I'm not supposed to tell you that," she says, "because you'll tell the social worker."

Katherine, realizing the child's dilemma, asks, "How do you like your teacher this year?"

Relieved, Faye says, "She's nice." She chats on about her reading class, and Katherine recalls Faye's mother saying in her first talk with her, "I'm a good mother. I don't know why they don't believe that. I am a good mother."

Katherine sighs to herself, "Maybe, just someone who never learned how to love a child."

Kids learn about love from you as they observe it in your commitment to caring for them.

. . . don't pray when it rains if you don't pray when the sun shines.

— SATCHEL PAIGE

The four children and I search the yard looking for our beloved cat.

"Here, kitty, kitty," calls four-year-old Atyssia sadly. "Where are you? We're all worried sick."

Kitty jumps out of the window well, dry leaves and pine needles matted in her fur.

Atyssia claps her hands and squeals, "I see her! I see her! Alleluia! This is the best ever day!"

You teach children to celebrate life's rays of sunshine. They are happier people because you help them find the silver linings when life looks gray.

A little madness in the Spring is wholesome even for the King.

— EMILY DICKINSON

Roy, the school custodian, tells the kids his pet, a long-haired, fifteen-pound, gold-colored cat with amber eyes, is Purrsy, the Cat King. Roy brings Purrsy to and from work every day. Today, when it's time to go home, Roy can't find the cat.

He searches frantically until a teacher says, "The after-schoolers asked if they could take him out on the playground. I didn't think you'd mind."

"No way," Roy says. "Purrsy's afraid of the kids."

"But it's a nice spring day," the teacher says, "and he seemed very happy to go."

Roy rushes to where the kids have gathered and finds Purrsy riding down the slide on Betsy's lap. At the bottom, Purrsy jumps to Bruce who delightedly carries him back to the top. Purrsy and Bruce swish down, and Katie picks Purrsy up for another ride.

Astonished, Roy says, "What a story this makes! Disney, eat your heart out!"

You give kids the gift of fun and fantasy when you allow a little spring madness from which to create their own stories to savor and tell.

Nobody sees a flower—really—we haven't time—to see takes time.

— GEORGIA O'KEEFFE

"Sometimes I have to remind myself how new everything in the world is when you're a first grader," Bob told the center director.

"Like Jamie Wilson today," Bob continued. "He marveled over a new flower that opened on that plant in the window. He kept going over to it and exclaiming, 'It wasn't there yesterday.' After about six times, I wanted to say, 'So it wasn't there yesterday. Let's get back to work.' But seeing that kid rekindled in me the wonder of discovery we lose along the way.

Then I asked myself, 'What difference does it really make if we don't do the work we planned to do?' The answer was, 'no difference.' We all needed to stop and talk about that flower—how it happened to be there today—even though it wasn't there yesterday."

You encourage healthy curiosity about the world and make kids feel important because you take the time to share their discoveries.

Unfolding from the first word,
The story of a child is read on the horizon of possibility.
Like a sunrise colored by many dreams
We welcome this beginning for our children . . .

— MARY WYNNE

"I would be honored to come," I said when Lidia's mother invited me to the new baby's welcoming day.

"Be there before sunrise," she warned me.

"I'll be there. Thank you again."

As I drove in the morning dark, I remembered when I first came to this beautiful place. Somewhat reluctantly, these Hopi parents allowed me to care for their children while they worked. My Hopi grandmother instilled in me respect for my heritage. Still, I knew more about the ways of New York City and had much to learn about my culture.

The women who walk with the baby to greet the sun rising above the copper horizon stood together. Lidia's mother saw me and said, "Because you listen with an open heart, you may come with us. Today we will give the baby your grandmother's name because she brought you to our children."

Your respectful caring encourages families to share with you the brightest part of their lives—the endless possibilities that they hold for their children.

Every day's a kick!
— OPRAH WINFREY

Joline, a preschool teacher, spent the entire week talking about spring, animals, and rebirth in nature with her three year olds. She read them Eric Carle's *The Very Hungry Caterpillar*, and completed the lessons with a fascinating puppet show about cocoons and butterflies.

On Monday, Nikki's mother stopped Joline in the hall. She told Joline that when she had driven Nikki home from preschool on Friday night, they had seen a dead raccoon lying on the side of the highway. Nikki had blurted out, "Oh, Mama, that poor raccoon! Now, he'll never be a butterfly."

"Oh well, raccoon-cocoon," Joline laughed, "Some concepts just don't take the first time around."

Your sense of humor is a real asset for kids because you manage to laugh and teach, with patience, the lessons they need repeated again and again.

Dissension is healthy, even when it gets loud.

— JENNIFER LAWSON

The three one year olds sat in a row in their high chairs. As they put most—or rather some—of the macaroni and cheese in their mouths, they carried on their conversations. Yee Lee burped.

"Me burp," he announced proudly.

"Daddy burp," Quincy said.

"No," shouted Rollie, "My daddy burp."

Yee banged his spoon and cried, "No, Mama burp."

The crying and banging racket started to irritate five-year-old Mari. "Okay, babies," she said with sympathy and understanding. "Quiet down. I'm sure all of your parents are very good burpers."

You know that it's important to let children express their points of view and sometimes the discussions make you laugh, even if they get a little loud.

What is destructive is impatience, haste.

— MAY SARTON

After 4:30 p.m., tension builds as adults hurry in to pick up kids. Lucia says to her dad, "You need to sign my permission slip for the trip to the zoo."

"I'll do it in the morning. Get your coat," he says.

"You have to do it tonight," Lucia insists.

"Okay, where is it?" her dad asks, impatiently.

"I'll get it," Lucia says and goes to find her teacher.

"Hey, Lucia," Ginger calls from across the room.

Lucia sidetracks to meet Ginger. The two nine year olds talk fast about plans for tomorrow. When Lucia sees her dad coming, she scoots toward her teacher. Her dad follows.

"My dad needs a consent form and pen, quick," Lucia says rapidly and zips on by. The teacher steps forward to meet Lucia's dad.

"Here's the form, Mr. Bronn, and a pen," she says.

He moves to a table, bends, and signs his name.

Lucia returns with her coat on, takes her dad's hand, looks up at her teacher, and says, "Whew. Thanks."

Your empathy with kids is a special gift they know they can count on when other adults act with haste and impatience.

Take no thought of the harvest
But only of proper sowing.

— T. S. ELIOT

Seven-month-old Vanessi wants me to carry her all of the time these days. The frustration and joy of taking care of infants is that they go through stages so fast. It seems that I just blink and they are different people. It's hard to know what to expect.

The good part is I don't have to worry too much that I will spoil them or do the wrong thing because their needs change so quickly. So I'll keep Vanessi strapped to my back or next to my heart every waking moment this week. Next week she'll need something else and she'll tell me what that is and I will listen.

When you carry children next to your heart and listen to their needs, you sow the seeds for children to have healthy, secure lifetimes.

Every child is an artist. The problem is how to remain an artist when he grows up.

Jason's dad greets him with a playful karate move when he comes for him after school. Jason returns the mock motion. Dad musses his hair. They tussle a few seconds.

Dad asks, "How'd it go, guy?" Jason talks about a soccer game or the computer but never mentions his favorite place, the art corner. He hurries to it every day where he works on a collage, using paper textures, shapes, and colors of his choice.

One day a dazzling kaleidoscope emerges that seems to move on the page. The teacher admiringly holds it up for all to see. "Your dad's going to love this," she says.

Jason takes it from her hands, puts it on the worktable, and quietly says, "No he won't. He'll say it's girls' stuff."

When you help young hands create, you free minds and hearts from stereotypes into which the world would lock their spirit.

The children dance and the grown people get dizzy.
— MALAGASY PROVERB

"Faster, faster," said Gareth, the leader of the imaginary horses. "We will run up these mountains and then we can munch grass in the field."

Gareth and his "horses" galloped up one park hill and pranced down the other. Patsy, their caregiver, tried to keep up but was starting to feel lost in the dust.

Gareth, often as thoughtful as he is creative, saw her panting. "Whoa, horsies," he said, "there's an old donkey who wants to play with us. Let's let her catch up."

You encourage children's imaginations to dance in worlds full of fantasy and fun. What beautiful childhood memories they will have because you agree to go along for the spinning ride.

To feel valued, to know, even if only once in awhile, that you do a job well is an absolutely marvelous feeling.

— BARBARA WALTERS

When Myrna's father died, she asked parents to find other child care for a week. She needed more time than just the day of his burial. Though unscheduled breaks in child care are a hassle to parents, they expressed their sympathy and managed.

The week passed. They came back. Kids stayed and parents left as though there had been no break at all until Myrna opened the door to Amy. Eyes sparkling, face aglow, clutching a bouquet of daisies, the three year old said, "For you."

When parents are late to pick up kids, the weather's too hot, wet, or cold, kids are cranky, or whenever you doubt the worth of your job, reflect on the "Amy days" you meet.

Those who do not know how to weep with their whole heart don't know how to laugh either.

— GOLDA MEIR

Jodie and Moira, both nine years old, threw punches and insults. A frustrated aide ushered them into the director's office.

"I hate you!" shrieked Jodie.

"My mother says you're a brat!" yelled Moira. "I never got in trouble before I knew you."

Both girls vented angrily but the bottom line was, as Jodie said, "We're losers, stuck with each other."

Frannie, the director, said, "I don't know for sure, but I think I hear two smart, good friends who take a lot of grief from other kids. Good guess?"

Moira rolled her eyes and threw her arm over the back of the chair. Jodie let tears stream down her cheeks and reached over to tenderly squeeze Moira's hand. "I love you, weirdo," she sobbed.

Returning the squeeze, Moira chuckled, "Everybody's a little weird. We're just good at it."

Because you take the time to get to the bottom line, kids learn how to live with their whole hearts.

Always leave them laughing when you say good-bye.
— GEORGE MICHAEL COHAN

The four year olds in Shirley's home care group, Allan, Mike, and Evie, are having a push-shove argument about Randy's birthday lunch.

The birthday child gets to choose a favorite food, and Randy opts for Raisin Bran cereal. The other three want spaghetti. Discussion rises to shouting pitch. Randy won't give in. Evie, standing her ground, screeches over and over, "Raisin Bran's for breakfast. Who ever heard of Raisin Bran for lunch?"

The fracas calms. But for the rest of the day, Evie demands to know from anyone who comes to the door, "Did you ever hear of Raisin Bran for lunch?"

By day's end, Shirley envisions an adult Evie out in the world, knocking on doors, taking her survey, "Have you ever heard of Raisin Bran for lunch?" And she laughs as Evie leaves for home.

When you find humor in trying, childish skirmishes, you ease tension and teach compromise—a valuable skill children learn from you.

Truly great people emit a light that warms the hearts of those around them.

— BANANA YOSHIMOTO

One hand clutched his newly adopted mother's skirt. The other held the orange poppy that he brought his teachers. Four-year-old Joseph lived in Korea a week ago. Now he was in a child care center where no one spoke his first language and few people had his beautiful dark skin and shiny black hair.

On the classroom door, pictures of Korean people and a "Welcome Joseph!" sign greeted him. He still hid behind his mother's leg. As his teacher, a white-haired, smiling-eyed person came closer, Joseph tugged at his mother's sleeve.

"What is it, honey?" she asked, surprised to see a relieved grin on his face.

"Honemi," he whispered. "Honemi."

"Honemi means grandmother," his mom told the teacher who bent down to accept the bright flower from her new friend.

Children respond to the warmth of your caring presence. To them you are one of the world's truly great people.

MAY 12

Challenges make you discover things about yourself
that you never really knew. They're what make
the instrument stretch—what make you go beyond
the norm.

— CICELY TYSON

Marion Marsh promises she'll give two-month-old Richie his bath and breakfast because Debbie, a first-time mom, is nervous about every phase of baby care.

Richie blossoms under Marion's care for three months, until the day Debbie arrives early to pick him up. Marion, sitting on a thick quilt on the living room floor with Richie, calls for Debbie to come in.

Richie, furiously working his arms and legs, is trying to roll over toward the toy rabbit in Marion's hand. Debbie gasps in horror, snatches Richie from the quilt, and says, "I don't want my baby on the floor, ever!"

Whenever you face up to those who challenge your expertise with children and teach the inexperienced, you help kids.

To love is to make of one's heart a swinging door.

— HOWARD THURMAN

Candre does child care and foster care. Kindle is one of the kids in her care. He's been coming to Candre's house since he was a year old. Four years old now, he knows the ABCs, his address, and how to tie his shoes, almost.

When Candre tells Kindle's mom, Sara, that a new foster baby is coming, Sara says, "I've thought of doing that, but I could never let them go. I guess I'm just too soft. How do you say good-bye to them after you've given them all that love?"

"Same way I say good-bye to Kindle every night," she says, wrapping him up in a big hug. "With a heart full of love." Gently closing the door behind Kindle she says, "Night, baby. See you tomorrow."

Many children come in and out of your life. You cherish them, and then let them go on their way with lots of love in your heart and often a tear in your eye.

We live in a society where people who don't earn money don't count.

— Cathleen Rountree

"Sometimes it reminds me of kids with their noses pressed against the window of a candy store. Those that can buy, get to go in; the others yearn for what's inside," says the Montessori school director. She's explaining to the church board what is happening in the under-used elementary school that houses the Montessori program.

"Maria Montessori rescued urchins off the street," the director pointed out, "and here we are, at least a century later, still trying to do that. But, unfortunately, what's happened is that no one is willing to pay the freight, so to speak.

"It's the old cliché, 'Them that has gets.' Montessori's become an elitist program in the United States. I don't think we have to let that continue. So I'm appealing again for a sliding fee scale and scholarship money so we can serve all kids, certainly those our program is meant for."

Your perseverance in treating all children equally in their eagerness for life holds out hope that someday money won't determine who gets a chance at tomorrow.

The sky blesses me, the earth blesses me. Up in the skies I cause the spirits to dance. On the earth, the people I cause to dance.

— CREE ROUND DANCE SONG

The five children huddled together on the glassed-in porch. Outside the thunder rolled and the lightning spiked. "Ohhhh, that was a scary one," says four-year-old Chad.

"Ah, don't be scared," says Noah. "My grandma says those are the angels rockin' and rollin'. She says if we rock and roll too, the storm stops faster."

With a little tremble in his voice, Chad asks, "Anybody want to dance?"

You encourage the spirit that causes children to dance. They can rock and roll bravely because they feel safe in your loving care.

*It's the song ye sing, and the smiles ye wear, that's a-
makin' the sun shine everywhere.*

— JAMES WHITCOMB RILEY

"Old MacDonald Had a Farm" spins on the
turntable. The kids, in a chain of ten, do a small-fry
version of the bunny hop, loudly oinking and
mooing as the lyrics demand, just as David's uncle
Mike comes to pick him up.

Mike leaves his dripping umbrella outside and
steps in. The kids prance past him, eyes shining,
heads dipping from side to side, small feet kicking
first to the left, and then to the right. David swings
by Mike and throws his uncle an extra wiggle and
a "Cha, cha, cha!" Mike laughs, "You'd never know
in here that it's gloomy out there."

**When you introduce kids to music and let them dance,
you give them sunshine to brighten a gloomy day.**

Whoever wants to be admired at a festival, should be prepared to dance well.

— IBO PROVERB

Six-year-old Gretchen loves to dance and spins to music when she thinks no one is watching. When the after-school program planned a talent show, Gretchen's teacher, Rosela, asked, "Why aren't you signed up, Gretchen?"

"I can't do anything."

"It looks like you can dance to me."

"Everyone says I look stupid. Even my mom."

"I know a little about dancing," said Rosela. "We could work up a routine. It's all in the practicing. You can do it."

For a month Gretchen practiced with Rosela. At home, she practiced in her room with the music turned down low. When the big day arrived, Gretchen shivered with fear. When she got on stage, however, she practically floated. During the applause, Gretchen saw her mother standing, smiling and clapping.

Backstage, Rosela wanted to hug Gretchen, but Gretchen ran off, looking for mom and throwing a "Thanks a lot," over her shoulder.

As kids learn who they are, your support gives them what it takes to show their talents to the world.

No one can make you feel inferior without your consent.

— ELEANOR ROOSEVELT

Julie, a toddler teacher, works at a child care center near the university where she is a senior. The kids love the games she plays and the stories she reads.

Julie puts her heart into teaching children. She even takes the toilet training chores, upchucking accidents, and spills that go along with toddler care, in her stride.

Most parents recognize that Julie is good at what she does. But when she told a dad the center would close for a day so the staff could attend a professional child care conference, his comment was, "You call this a profession?"

Caring for children is a vocation and a profession. Don't let careless, unappreciative comments affect your pride in what you do.

Invisibility is not a natural state for anyone.

— MITSUYE YAMADA

When Gabriella took the kids for a walk, baby Tiera took in the sights. As they waited for the light, Tiera looked up and down at the larger-than-life poster of the local TV news team on the bus stop glass. Gabriella watched her scanning the photo of four, thin, handsome white people.

"Don't you worry, baby," she said. "We'll teach you about lots of important people with skin as lovely dark brown as yours. You can be sure of that."

You build children's self-esteem and understanding when you teach them that real life pictures come in many beautiful, living colors.

*Good teaching is one-fourth preparation and
three-fourths theatre.*

— GAIL GOODWIN

Every Friday in Sheila's preschool class, one child is star for a day. This Friday is Tanya's day. The classroom bulletin board displays pictures of her and her family and a sign reads, "Meet Tanya, Star for a Day."

Born in Hawaii of Japanese parents, the shy four year old, who is new to the class, has chosen her grandma as her special guest. Tanya's grandma brings a videotape, book, and a gray-white puppy puppet named Tag-Along. The tape shows Hawaiian dances of joy. While grandma gives a tour of the islands with the oversized picture book, Tag-Along wags his tail, rolls his eyes, and perks his ears in response.

The enthralled kids applaud and laugh at Tag-Along's antics. Afterward, all excited, they gather around a smiling Tanya who now knows she belongs.

Be proud of the scripts you write and the stage you direct that allows kids to stand in the spotlight and shine.

*Don't be afraid to cry. It will free your mind of
sorrowful thoughts.*

— DON TALAYESVA

Petri skidded into first base and got one of
those stinging scrapes that have little stones in
them. He tried to stop crying. Taking big gasps of
air, he sobbed, "Boys don't cry. Boys don't cry."

"Well, I cry," said Ali, cleaning out the wound as
gently as possible. "And most of the guys I know
are smart enough to cry when things hurt. You're
a smart guy, so let it all come hollerin' out."

Kids learn from you that everything they hear isn't
necessarily true. They learn to live healthier lives
because you teach them to free their spirits.

To be alone is to be different; to be different is to be alone.

— SUZANNE GORDON

"Do you see any games to play alone?" the boy in the wheelchair asks Peg who is with the kids in her care at the toy warehouse.

"Let's look in the game section. It's right here," she answers. The kids pitch in, and soon the boy is laughing at their choices. "I'm a little old for Candyland," he says.

When his father appears, Peg learns that the boy's name is Peter and he is nine years old. Peter attends a mainstream school but spends many after-school hours alone.

"Do you think you'd like to get involved with these kids?" Peg asks. "They'd love to learn some new games."

"Could I do that, Dad?" Peter asks.

"Can he come with us now?" the kids want to know.

"Do you have time to talk about it now?" Peter's dad asks.

Peg replies, "Sure. We'll all get acquainted and work this out."

"Yippee!" the kids shout and scamper after Peter, wheeling his way toward the exit.

Your compassion brings a much-needed quality to a world where those who are different are too often alone.

*In general, I am not impressed by grand solutions. If
people start, in a small way, on their own front step, they
come to realize that big problems have small solutions.*

— MAGGIE KUHN

Three of us lived within a two-block area.
We all started doing child care about the same
time. Sometimes we sat on my front steps while
the kids rode their Big Wheels and trikes. We
shared concerns about children and our families.
A common theme was our low pay.

Taking a rest from peddling, Jared stopped by us
and heard our conversation. "My mom says you're
worth a million bucks," he said. "Get it!"

Lots of parents think you're fantastic! The problem
is they're often so busy they forget to tell you.
The solution might be to ask for some kind words
and, maybe, a portion of that million bucks!

This I would like to be—just a bit truer, less of the wisher
and more of the doer.

— EDGAR A. GUEST

Visitors at the history center gather around the roped-off area in the colonial village. An actor in early-American farmer's garb demonstrates how to card wool. He rubs the wool, which eventually becomes material for clothing, over the tool in his hand and shows the crowd how it begins to soften.

As he works and talks, a small voice repeats, "Wanta touch it. Wanta touch it." The farmer tries ignoring the interruptions, but finally looks down into the upturned face of two-year-old Casey, who is there with a group of toddlers and their teachers from a nearby nursery school. When the farmer puts the wool into Casey's curious hands, other kids and adults ask for some too.

While the colonial wife distributes pieces of wool, her husband lifts a beaming Casey over the rope barrier and says, "Meet Casey the wool-toucher, my apprentice for the day."

Because you're more of a doer than a wisher, you give kids experiences that will make them the doers of their future, your legacy to their world.

*I get energy from the earth itself, and I get optimism
from the earth itself. I feel that as long as the earth can
make a spring every year, I can.*

— ALICE WALKER

We moved from our big city condo to an old
house surrounded by acres of farmland dotted
with cows and cornstalks.

I got a teaching position at a nursery school next
to a shimmering blue lake in the middle of the
woods. Everything was new to me. I didn't know if
the pet goats were playing or charging. The singing
insects scared me. When the kids planted a garden,
I followed as they planted seeds in the toughs of
sandy dirt. We carefully labeled each row, "beans,"
"radishes," "cabbage." I thought I acted as if I knew
what I was doing, and I felt my homesickness
healing in the spring sun.

One morning, all of the labeled sticks
disappeared, blown away by the thunderwinds
the night before. As we knelt by the garden, four-
year-old Calvin whispered to me, "Don't worry,
I know what's the beans and what's the corn.
I'll show you later."

**You give and take new energy and loving optimism
as you help children grow.**

*We must not, in trying to think about how we can make
a big difference, ignore the small daily differences we
can make . . .*

— MARIAN WRIGHT EDELMAN

"Karl said that if I didn't let him play with his
gun, he'd tell his dad on me," Monique, a child care
provider, told her husband. "And he did tell on me.
Karl's dad said the gun was just a toy."

"I told him, 'Sorry, but I believe guns encourage
violence in children.' I told him that national
studies show homicide is the leading cause of
death for elementary and middle school children.
Some, like Karl, are only five years old.

"Marian Edelman, founder of the Children's
Defense Fund, says we have to remind people that
in the United States, every two hours, a child dies of
gunfire, equaling a classroom of kids every two
days. So I reminded Karl's dad.

"I didn't have a clue how he would react.
I thought he'd be angry. Instead, can you believe
he said, 'Thanks, Karl won't be playing with guns
anymore'? I feel like dancing!"

**The daily differences you make in the lives of children
are testimony to the love that could change our
violent world.**

Unshackled from the myth that nothing works,
we can assure that children without hope today
will have a real chance to become the contributing
citizens of tomorrow.

— LISBETH B. SCHOOR

Evelyn's first teaching position was at one of the "toughest" schools in town. The principal met her with her supplies: two erasers, chalk, and a paddle.

"I won't be needing this," Evelyn said, handing back the paddle.

"You'll learn. Nothing else works," the principal said.

Evelyn made other things work. She bought supplies and tutored free on weekends. She organized parents to storm the school board until the class size was reduced from 35 to 25. Her room was a beehive of learning centers and the first graders' test scores went up 20 points. Unfortunately, Evelyn burned out in four years and resigned.

The day she left, a mom waited for her in the parking lot. Giving Evelyn a carnation, she said, "Thanks for teaching Jesse to read. Thanks for giving us hope."

MAY 28

You are a hope giver who knows what children need. Your work today gives children a real chance for successful tomorrows.

Children need and want adults to set limits and rules.

— DAVID ELKIND

Jody, 7, jumps from her swing at the after-school club's picnic. She tells her nine-year-old sister, Carolyn, that she's going to the rest room and starts toward a building across the road. Her teacher calls her back. "We'll all go over together in just a few minutes, Jody," her teacher says.

"I can go by myself. It's just across over there," Jody says, pointing to the green wooden building.

"Sorry," the teacher says, "But we'll go together."

Jody plunks down on a bench. "Can't even go to the bathroom by myself," she sulks angrily.

"Come on, Jody, lots of strangers come to parks," Carolyn says. "She just doesn't want to see your face on a milk carton, okay?"

When you have to hold firm and allow kids no choice, you show them a love they'll come to understand and depend on.

And thus, dear children, have ye made for me this
day a jubilee.
— HENRY WADSWORTH LONGFELLOW

Golden balloons shine in the afternoon sun.
Miss Genevieve's party, held in honor of her fifty
years of teaching, is in full swing. All dressed up in
a suit, George, the school custodian, asks to say a
few words. He often teaches the junior high boys
how to shoot baskets and repair things. They listen
as their six-foot-four hero speaks.

"Miss G. was my fifth-grade teacher. I thank you,
Miss G.," he says with a tear in his voice, "for
teaching me to always be kind." Then he bends
over and gives her a kiss.

Without speaking, the boys one by one kiss
Miss G. on the cheek and whisper, "Thank you."

Many lives are richer because of your loving care.
Many hearts whisper, "Thanks," and give special
honor to you.

MAY 30

Children of life are we, as we stand with our lives uncarved before us.

— GEORGE WASHINGTON DOANE

They stand at Gate 12, nervously awaiting the plane bringing them a baby daughter from a faraway land.

They are a working couple. Their son, Roddy, is a happy, well-adjusted four year old who has been going to a child care center since he was five months old. The couple has arranged for the same infant care for their daughter to start in three months.

As they wait, they reassure themselves about plans for the new life that's about to join theirs.

"It'll be wonderful," they say, hurrying to meet the social worker walking toward them—ready to take into their hearts a little girl whose journey has not ended but just begun.

Because you give children love and care, you are part of the hope that a kinder world stands ready to receive them.

Money will buy a pretty good dog, but it won't buy the wag of his tail.

— JOSH BILLINGS

Kids arrive at the Johnson's starting about 7 a.m., tightly grasping small plastic bags of treats for Polly, the child care dog.

But Polly's missing; somehow she's gotten out of the fenced yard.

"Can't we go find her?" the kids plead.

"We'll watch for her on our morning walk," Edith Johnson says.

No one sees her. At story time, the doorbell rings. Edith opens the door to a police officer and a leashed gray, white, and black shaggy dog. Tail down, it looks sad as only a multi-breed mutt can.

"This your dog?" the officer asks. The kids run from the story circle, jumping, clapping, and shouting, "Polly's home!" The dog perks her ears, woofs loud greetings, and wags her tail like a windshield wiper on high speed. Over the din, Edith says, "Sorry, I didn't hear you. What did you ask?"

Money can't buy moments of love and joy that nurture kids and make your work invaluable.

There is no frigate like a book to take us miles away.

— EMILY DICKINSON

"Buenos Dias, Marguerita," says Roberta, a child care provider.

"Buenos Dias," the shy six year old softly replies.

Uncle Luis apologizes that Marguerita missed the morning bus and leaves her with a hug, admonishing her to "Go play. Have fun."

Marguerita dashes off to the play area where the kids in the summer school age program flip on the monkey bars and take turns on the swings and slides. After a picnic lunch, Roberta reads *Candles on the River* to them.

The picture book tells about the Mexican custom of floating candles on the river toward loved ones far away; and, for a while, the children are miles from the migrant-worker poverty they know.

But when the bus arrives to take them back to their families, they eagerly scramble on board, waving and calling out, "Gracias," until the bus is out of sight.

Though you can't rescue children from poverty, you help them rise above its shadow when you nurture their spirit.

JUNE 2

We must concentrate on what we can do and erase "can't," "won't," and "don't think so" from our vocabulary.

— CARDISS COLLINS

Sylvia takes care of children with special physical needs. She dreamt of opening a camp for the kids where they could enjoy sunshine and friends, but she didn't think she had the time, the know-how, or the money. She often told her dream to her best friend, Lorraine, who would laugh, "Talk, talk, talk. Girl, I'm going to live to see you catch your rainbow."

One day Lorraine called and said, "I got some bad news. I've got cancer and it doesn't look good. Shocker, huh? I've thought about what I want to get done and I want to help you with your dream."

"I can't let you do that," Sylvia gasped. But, of course, she did.

The camp opened a month after Lorraine died. Sylvia helped the kids get off the buses and whispered, "We did it! Thanks, Girl!"

What you do each day, most people couldn't begin to do. You can grab your rainbow dream, large or small, and make it happen; you can begin today.

We must have a place . . . where children can have a whole group of adults they can trust.

— MARGARET MEAD

Linked together with colorful ribbon-like rope, the kids in the downtown child care center walk along in pairs, eliciting smiling attention from passersby. The three teachers point out items of interest as the group makes its way to visit a high-rise for the elderly.

Three-year-old Betsy, in her Annie Hall hat with the large pink rose, is especially friendly. She can't resist waving and smiling, enticing people to stop to talk to her. When they do, she puts her head down, walks a little faster, and never speaks. Gus, her teacher, quietly explains, "I guess she's shy."

After several such encounters, Betsy looks up at him and whispers apologetically, "My mommy told me not to talk to strangers."

He pats her shoulder and says, "I know, Betsy. I know."

The safety you offer kids frees them to do what their hearts naturally do—simply trust.

Nothing cures like time and love.

— LAURA NYRO

Gillian pitches stones in a corner of the yard.

"Mad at somebody?" I ask.

"Not really," he answers.

"Another problem you want to talk about?"

"Not really."

"Okay," I say, and continue to plant the pansies.

"Well...my cat, Clancy, died last night."

"I'm sorry. How did he die?"

"It was a she and she was hit by a car."

"Can I help?"

"Only good old father time can do that," says the little philosopher, pitching stones in a corner of the yard.

You are there for children, and as wise as they may be, they still appreciate your supportive heart.

Love and laughter hold us together.

Every child visits the bathroom before going outdoors. That's a rule. Molly and Felice monitor the activity, making sure the children wash their hands.

Ann Louise, three years old, argues, in the way kids have of confusing time, "I don't have to go. I went yesterday."

After convincing her to try, Felice says to Molly, "That reminds me of a cartoon I saw in a parenting book. The dad tells the little boy to use the rest room before they leave the 'Last Chance' gas station on a vacation trip.

"'I don't hafta,' the boy says.

"'Are you sure?' the dad asks.

"The boy says, 'I'm sure.'

"Halfway up into a mountain range, from the back of the overloaded family wagon, a little voice says, 'Now, I hafta.'"

"So Ann Louise," Molly laughs, "Now you hafta."

Your ability to meet, with humor, the challenges kids present shows them the patience and love that holds their world together.

There's a period of life when we swallow a knowledge of ourselves and it becomes either good or sour inside.

— PEARL BAILEY

Sophie was the local child care center before the term was invented. Mothers in her neighborhood worked before society admitted that mothers worked. These mothers cleaned houses, curled hair, and "helped out" at their husbands' shops. Sophie taught school, but when her son developed arthritis, she stayed home and the children came to her. She spent most of her time proving to them how smart they were.

"You are somebody," she would say.

Sophie's retired now but she still hears from many kids that she cared for.

"Thanks, Sophie," they say, "for helping me to believe that I am somebody. It made all the difference."

You are connected to a long line of people who made a difference in children's lives. You can be proud of your profession and the life-building work you do.

We have one simple rule here: Be kind.

— SAM JAFFEE

Ruby's mom rented an apartment for them near Ruby's school. The school requires that kids who live close enough to walk to school go home for lunch. Ruby couldn't do that because her mom works. The school principal referred Ruby and her mom to Mary Lee who does family child care.

"It's hard enough for Ruby to be the new kid on the block without this," her worried mom told Mary.

"She'll be fine," Mary assured her. "We'll do lunch, won't we, Ruby?"

Ruby liked doing lunch at Mary's and made friends with other "walkers." But on the last day of school, she arrived in tears. "I can't go back," she said. "I don't have a present for my teacher, and all the other kids do."

"Don't cry sweetie," Mary said, "we'll get Grandma Wilson next door to stay with you kids while I go get a box of candy for your teacher."

Later, with a gaily wrapped package firmly in hand, Ruby skipped down the walk away from Mary Lee.

Never doubt the lasting influence of kindness you give to kids even when you but briefly touch their lives.

Be happy. It is a way of being wise.

— COLETTE FRENCH

Monica directs the only child care center in a small town. Everyone goes to her when they don't know what to do about terrible twos, toilet training, or a hundred other problems. People usually leave her office with a solution and a smile.

Mike's four year old goes to Monica's center. One day, after half an hour of discussing what to do about his son's new fascination with bad words, Mike says, "I don't know if you're as smart as folks think you are or if you just make people feel a whole lot better."

"Can't lose either way, can I?" Monica said, smiling, "Have a good one!"

You wisely support parents as you work together for the children. Families are fortunate to have your good advice, giving spirit and sense of humor to help them along.

Yesterday I dared to struggle. Today I dare to win.

— BERNADETTE DEVLIN

Toni, smiling and sobbing, accepts a dozen roses from her best friend while her proud grandmother holds tiny Liza. Less than a year ago the now triumphant seventeen year old had stood before a packed school board meeting, scared, trembling, begging for this chance.

"My grandma raised me after my mom left," she had told the board. "I owe it to her to take care of myself. The student council proposal before you for a nursery at the high school is a plea from me and others like me.

"As the proposal says, private money will pay for the child care people who will also teach parenting. Churches will help, and students will volunteer time. We can make this work."

People over-shouted Toni's testimony, "You'll just make it easier to have more babies." The chair's gavel banged repeatedly for order. Finally, with child caregivers leading the way, and teachers, pastors, parents, and grandparents supporting it, the proposal passed, signaling hope.

You give courage to young people just by being who you are, a person who cares about kids in a world struggling to win a better tomorrow.

We may misunderstand, but we do not misexperience.

— VINE DELORIA

Simone put out the color mixing materials. She stirred paints, cleaned containers, put a layer of plastic under everything, and made sure there were enough waterproof smocks. She didn't finish until 7 p.m.

"Maybe next time I'll just pass out the markers," she thought wearily.

The next day, three-year-old Jessica poured water, a little yellow, and some green in a tube. "Look!" she exclaimed. "I made the sky!"

Your dedication and creative work give children the gift of discovery. Children's lives are full of rich, lasting experiences that light up their learning for a lifetime.

Every survival kit should include a sense of humor.

— U<small>NKNOWN</small>

Beatrice wants the kids in her care to experience neighborhood living, so kids from the neighborhood often come to play. But she has a rule that parents must call first.

This week her father is visiting. Mel, a five year old who lives nearby, comes into the yard where grandpa has stretched out in the hammock after lunch while the kids are napping. Mel stands close to the hammock, staring curiously at grandpa's bald head.

When Beatrice comes outside, Mel whispers hoarsely, "What happened to his hair?" At that, grandpa opens one eye and says, "Son, I think your mother wants you."

Mel bends over the hammock and says, "No she doesn't. She sent me here."

Mel's comment that his mother had sent him jolts Beatrice some. It meant his mom had violated Beatrice's "call first" rule; but the scene is so funny Beatrice has to laugh along with the boy and her dad.

Your sense of humor and love for kids are your survival for times when your work can make you vulnerable to the unfair behavior of others.

Today we are blessed with this beautiful baby. May her feet be to the east, her right hand to the south, her head to the west, her left hand to the north. May she walk and dwell on Mother Earth peacefully.

— NAVAJO CHILD BLESSING PRAYER

Elliot's mom had a baby. The children and I went to the hospital and Elliot's mom brought the baby, wrapped in a fuzzy green blanket, to the window. We waved and cooed. On the way home, Amanda began crying.

"What's wrong?" I asked.

"Poor Elliot's baby," she sobbed. "It only has a head."

We went home and practiced wrapping dolls up in fuzzy blankets and talked about how much fun it will be to count the new baby's fingers and toes.

You lead children to appreciate the beautiful gift of life and guide them gently down the path of understanding. Your patience brings them peace.

It ain't no use putting up your umbrella 'til it rains.

— ALICE CALDWELL RICE

"There's no seat for me," says six-year-old Marianne, waiting in the bus line for her first day in the summer school age program.

"Right here, behind me," the driver says, helping her aboard.

At the center, Barb, the teacher, says, "Just in time for snacks."

"What if there's no place for me?" Marianne asks.

"There is," Barb replies, leading her to the bin with her name on it and waiting while she shelves her book bag. In the snack room, Barb guides Marianne to a table and says to the kids there, "This is Marianne. Let's welcome her."

Janie and Krista move to make room. Susie opens a milk carton for her, and Andy gives her a straw. Barb hovers near for a while.

"Wanta play supermarket?" Janie asks. "You can be cashier, 'cause it's your first day."

Marianne nods shyly, bites into her cookie, and sips her milk. The kids all talk at once, explaining how the market works. Barb moves on.

Your ability to foresee what worries kids folds their cares away like the umbrella they don't need 'til it rains.

*Beauty in its truest form, is seeing the world through
my child's eyes: seeing the excitement, the wonder,
and the innocence. When I allow myself to do that,
I am my happiest.*

— LAURIE NUMEDAHL-MEUWISSEN

"You are too grumpy today, Millie," Torry said,
folding her arms and frowning.

"I'm just busy. Sometimes big people get very
busy," Millie answered. "Why don't you run outside
and enjoy the sunshine?"

"Why don't you run outside and enjoy me?"
Torry asks, skipping backward to the door,
beckoning with her index finger and the "I-know-
I've-got-you-now" grin.

Secure in your care, children invite you to join them in
seeing the world through their eyes. Aren't you glad
when you accept their wonderful invitation?

Learn to make the most of life. Lose no happy day!

— SARAH DOUDNEY

"Let me put the money in," squeals three-year-old Racine.

"Honey, you just ride," her mom says, lifting her onto the riding horse in front of the "By-The-Hour Kids Care Center."

Sharie and Frances, leaving work for the day, stop to watch the delighted youngster. Racine's mom turns to the two care providers and says, "Next we buy a book and stop by the pet store to see the kittens. One day a month we do what my daughter wants. She always chooses time with you. I get a lot done, but I can't wait to pick her up. I suppose I'm spoiling her. But it's the best day off I get."

"Sounds like a great plan to us," Sharie says.

Moving on, Frances comments, "The hardest thing about working with kids is not having control over what else happens to them. I love it when I see people spoiling them. I can't help it."

Happy times with you teach kids to make the most of each day, a lesson for living they take with them into the rest of their lives.

I believe there is a brief magical moment in every relationship when the right statement will change a life.

— L. TOBIN

Nine-year-old Tyrone rarely talks. Kids call him the zombie. Affirmations, charts, and encouragement didn't get any results. Yesterday, I saw Tyrone leaning on a wall. "Hi, Ty! Want to join us for kickball?" No response. The moment had come to risk something new.

"It's time you faced reality," I told him. "You can make some changes or choose to be miserable forever."

After work, I called my mother. "I think I've ruined a kid's life," I cried.

Today, Ty's dad stopped me, "I don't know what happened yesterday but Ty and I had a long talk. He wants to try. I thought you should know that everything you've done probably changed my son's life."

The possibility of changing lives is one that you continue to take seriously through study, heartfelt listening, and careful thought.

Oft a little morning rain foretells a pleasant day.

— CHARLOTTE BRONTË

Last Friday, Audrey picked up sixteen-month-old Christopher at her mom's. "I stopped at the child care center near work," Audrey told her mom, "and they have room for one toddler. Christopher can start Monday. That's a little sooner than we talked about, but he's too much for you now that he wants to explore the world."

Monday comes. Audrey leaves Chris crying for grandma, and she's miserable. On her afternoon break, she stands at the office window gazing worriedly down at the center's play area, not really seeing the kids until she recognizes Chris.

He's hurrying his little feet toward a rolling ball. He stops it and pitches it back at the teacher, throwing himself off balance and sitting down hard. Laughing, he puts his hands down in front of him, gives himself a push up, and goes for the ball again.

Just then Audrey's mother calls to ask how the new plan went.

With a smile in her voice, Audrey answers, "Unbelievably well. God bless child care!"

Your dependable expertise can make a rainy day sunny for parents who couldn't do their jobs without your support.

Nothing is achieved in a dream.

— MALINKE PROVERB

"Time to wake up," Elizabeth says, gently rousing the nappers.

A little later, crunching on an apple at snack time, Leon says, "I dreamed I was flying. I wish I could fly awake."

"When I was five years old," Elizabeth says, "I could fly. I know I could."

"Really?"

"Yep. I would go over to that hill in the park, that really tall one, close my eyes, run down with my arms like this," Elizabeth stretches her arms out like wings. "I'd say 'I'm flying' and run down fast and then I could fly."

"Really?"

"I think so. Do you want to try after snack, see if it works for you?"

Remembering what it was like to be a child, you enter the world of children's dreams and give them what they need to make them come true.

*Quick sensitiveness is inseparable from a ready
understanding.*

— JOSEPH ADDISON

Julia's grandson is missing. She is panicked and
on the phone to the emergency operator.

When the police arrive, she says anxiously, "I've
been right with him all morning. We played on the
swings in the park for a while and went to the
library. I helped him choose two books, and then
we went to the toy store. We picked out a gravel
truck. Then we came home.

"I went indoors to get lunch and left him busy
in the sandbox building a road. I was even helping
with that. He can't open the gate. But he's gone."

Just minutes after starting to search the
house and yard, an officer calls out, "Here's your
missing boy."

Julia hurries to where the officer is bending,
peering into the dimness under the back deck of
Julia's daughter's house. In the beam of a police
flashlight, curled up behind a crawl space Julia
didn't know about, was the precocious, weary, two
and a half year old.

"Grandma," he says, "I need some privacy."

**Your sensitivity is invaluable to kids who rely on you
to know their limits.**

The more we can love ourselves and attend to all of life around us with a loving, open, connected heart and good relationship, the more we can be in a beautiful place.

— BROOKE MEDICINE EAGLE

Pink strawberry blossoms, tiny blue forget-me-nots, sturdy black-eyed Susans, and lacy parsley plants dance in the view from the kitchen window. Sometimes a gopher, bunny, or goldfinch joins the scene.

"Should we go check on the garden after lunch?" Tracy asks the children as they munch veggies and bread and look out onto their backyard world.

Thoughtful Lizzy answers, "We better, or all those creatures will get too lonely."

Your attention to life creates a beautiful place for children filled with connected hearts and warm, open relationships.

The most sensitive, most delicate of instruments—the mind of a child!

— HENRY HANDEL RICHARDSON

After naptime, Sally, the teaching aide, hurries to get the three year olds, Connie, Sammy, and Erica, outside with the other kids, but independence reigns. Connie refuses help with her shoes. "I do myself," she says, pulling narrow leather straps toward buckles, again and again.

So Sammy decides he, too, will "do myself." He sits next to Connie, poking limp laces at shoe eyelets. Erica heads for the door, barefoot. Sally intercepts and says, "You can't go out without shoes."

When Connie joyously announces, "See! Did it myself!" Sammy allows Sally to help him, and Erica returns to the door carrying her sandals, ready to go (no one said she had to put them on).

While helping Erica into her sandals, Sally glances over at Connie. "Sweetie," she says softly, "your shoes are on the wrong feet." To which Connie replies, "They's the only feet I got."

Sally muffles a giggle, and, at last, they file outdoors.

Because of your patience and sensitivity, kids gain self-confidence, so vital to them in their quest for independence.

*. . . introduce me to a world where I don't have
to miss myself.*

— LESLIE REESE

Carefully, Jay taped the postcards with
children's beautiful faces of many hues down
low on the wall, right where the toddlers could
see them.

As the day began, parents arrived with their
beloved children. Jay greeted each child with a
hug and an "hola." When she stretched out her
arms to Delores, Delores toddled right past her to
the new pictures.

"Hermanas, hermanas," she said, patting the
pictures gently.

**The world you create for children is familiar and
welcoming. Children find themselves loved and
wanted in your thoughtful care.**

One of the luckiest things that can happen to you in life is, I think, to have a happy childhood.

— AGATHA CHRISTIE

The day is sunny and warm. Lunch at Jan Morris's child care home is outside. One-year-old Michele bounces in her kiddie seat. Kids at the picnic table sing "The Wheels on the Bus Go Round and Round," as Jan sets out paper plates.

Maggie, Debbie, and Paul, who live nearby, watch through the fence, whispering. "You ask, Debbie, you live closest," Maggie says.

"No, you ask," Debbie replies.

"I'll ask," Paul says. "Mrs. Morris, can we come for lunch too?"

Jan turns to her small charges and asks, "Should we have company for lunch?"

"Yeah," the kids shout and clap their hands.

"Go ask your moms. If they say it's all right, you're in," Jan says.

Minutes later they're back, two jubilant four year olds and beaming three-year-old Paul. Michele bounces a little faster, kids at the table make room for the newcomers, and lunch goes on amid childish giggles and chitchat.

The happy childhood times you create for kids are the memories they'll build on as they grow and look back with warm remembrance.

*Try this bracelet; if it fits you wear it; but if it hurts you,
throw it away no matter how shiny.*

— KENYAN PROVERB

As they twist blue, fuchsia, and gold strings into friendship bracelets, the children are learning how to be friends. These "bad" kids shove, talk back, and swear. Their bottom line is that they don't think much of themselves.

Jackie, the group leader, is trying to change all of that.

Corrine is having trouble making her bracelet. Throwing it, she shouts, "Stupid baby project. Who needs it anyway?" She stomps out.

"She's being dumb. Dumby girl," Anton chants.

"Anton, quick, say three good things about yourself," Jackie says.

"I'm good at pool. I'm cute. I'm smart."

"You're also kind and helpful."

Anton's eyes flash as he gets Jackie's point. He finds Corrine.

"All you do is pin one end of the bracelet down," Anton says. "Who's the lucky dude who gets this bracelet anyway?"

"It's not for a dude, stup—I mean, Anton," replies Corrine. "I'm making it for Jackie."

From you, children learn how to fit into the world. By recognizing the best in kids you teach them respect for themselves and others.

As a working mom you have so much guilt laid
upon you . . .

— A Working Mom

Sharon rushes in with her children, Erin and Shawn. "Could you give them breakfast?" she asks Emily, the child care provider. "Shawn's upset and wouldn't eat. So Erin wouldn't either."

"We'll manage," Emily says.

Once their mom is gone, Erin spoons away at her cereal. But Shawn storms on about his mother leaving him. He wants to stay home, swing on his own swing, dig in his own sandbox. "Why does she have to go to work anyway?" he asks.

Emily tells him that his mommy loves him and wants him to have good food and toys to play with. "Besides, I like having you come to my house," she says.

Shawn decides his juice looks good. But before he takes a sip, he says, "How come you don't work?"

When kids see only the care you give and not the work it involves, parents know they're little ones are in good hands, easing tension and unwarranted guilt.

Something used by someone else has a history with it.
A piece of cloth, a cut glass pitcher, a recipe.

— MICHELE CLIFF

"This is your classroom," the director proudly told Gwen, the new teacher. "State of the art. We have all of the latest equipment."

"It looks like a spaceship," thought Gwen. "I'll do something about all of that plastic and Formica counter top." She felt fortunate to get a job that paid almost a living wage, so she kept her comments to herself.

A month later, a grandmother came and made an old family recipe. "Doesn't it seem homey with the smell of cinnamon baking?" the grandmother asked.

"Yes, it sure does," answered Gwen, thoughtfully.

From that day forward, Gwen asked families to bring in things from home for the classroom. The kids helped lug in tablecloths, stuffed chairs, rugs, and baskets. They told stories of grandpa's lamp or aunt's lace dollies. Gwen was glad to be off the spaceship and the children were proud of the new sign on the door: "Welcome to the home that kids made."

Children feel at home in your thoughtful care because you encourage them to tell their stories and share pieces of their history.

The world tips away when we look into our children's faces.

— LOUISE ERDICH

The sturdy three-year-old twins stand in front of their mom commanding, "Mommy, watch!" Mom turns away from getting their coats and looks at them in wonderment. They move their chubby fingers in a crawling motion up from mid-chest to their foreheads and lisp out their version of "Itsy Bitsy Spider."

In keyless children's voices, they sing the story of the spider who goes up the water spout only to have the rain come and wash him out. When they reach "Out came the sun and dried up all the rain," their mom can resist no longer. Kneeling, she sweeps the two beaming little ones into her arms, looking as though they've captured the world.

Your work speaks for itself when the troubles of the world give way to the sparkle of achievement in a child's eyes.

The sun shines not on us, but in us.

— JOHN MUIR

From June through August almost every day is sunny in this beach town, so we planned a sand castle building day for the end of June. The kids spent weeks designing their castles. Working together, they sketched ideas on paper and made clay models.

Early in the evening before our long-awaited event, a freak storm blew in. Pouring rain and raging winds accompanied the glum children in the morning. But their faces lit up with surprise and delight when I opened the garage door. The floor was a huge sandpile that had been hauled in during the night by my husband, a landscaper. He stood there beaming and said, "I brought the beach to you. Go to it, kids."

You push the gloominess away for children when you teach them how to shine despite the clouds that get in their way.

*Better you should forget and smile, than that you
should remember and be sad.*

— CHRISTINA ROSSETTI

At a toy store in the mall, Christine met Estelle, a former neighbor whose child had been in her home care group from age six weeks to four years. They had moved when Estelle became a vice-president at her company.

Estelle's designer suit, fashionable pumps, just-right makeup, and hair style looked wonderful.

"Glad this is open evenings or I wouldn't have gotten here," Estelle said to Christine. "Can you believe Timmy's six? Have to get a present for him to take to a party. Always something." She pulled a children's video from the counter display.

"He's finally in school," she said, "but I'm still paying out for after-school care."

Gold card back in her wallet, Estelle picked up her package, and said hurriedly, "Nice to see you."

"Are you still baby-sitting?" she added. "Bye."

"Baby-sitting" is a thoughtless term for the professional care you give. Follow your heart, which makes you grateful for whatever helps toward the happiness of a child.

We are stardust. We are golden.

— JONI MITCHELL

"When I swish my magic wand, all bad things will go poof!"

"What will the world be like then?" I ask the five-year-old magic person.

Between a tiptoe and a wand wave, she replies, "Beautiful, like you."

You deserve golden moments—let their lovely magic live in your heart.

Give thanks for singers of lullabies, singers of nonsense, and small scraps of melody.

— MICHAEL LUNIG

On a walk with her young charges, Johanna sees Alicia, a neighbor and teenage mom, sitting on the front steps of the house where she lives with her grandma.

"Hey, Alicia," she says. "How's Tyrice?"

"He's why I'm out here," Alicia answers, her voice breaking. "Sometimes he cries so much. I get so nervous. I put him in his crib and sit here until I get it together again."

"Why don't you just bring him over to my house while your grandma's at work?" Johanna asks. "You can help with these kids, and I can help with your baby. Let's get him now. We'll leave a note for your grandma."

Johanna, holding Tyrice, sings "Hush, little baby. Don't you cry...," while Alicia writes the note and locks the door. The crying stops as the two women and five excited kids walk off to Johanna's house and a safe place for Tyrice.

Compassion is an invaluable gift you offer the world when you share your "song" with children.

I'm cautious about making money at something that is not the love of my life.

— EMILY PRAGER

Michael's mother came late, just as he was eating some rather messy spaghetti. "Oh, I'm so sorry," his mother said. "My boss handed me three hours worth of work at four o'clock and traffic was horrible."

We both helped Michael get his legs into a clean pair of overalls.

"What a day!" she sighed. "The coffee pot gossip says I'm not getting my promotion, my biggest account gave his business to his brother-in-law, and I have a headache that won't quit."

I tied Michael's shoes while she washed his face.

"Let's go, Mikey," she said to her son. "We have to stop at the grocery store and get your brother to hockey practice. Sorry, again, about being late. I don't know how you can stand taking care of these kids. You're a saint!"

If sainthood is awarded to those who love what they do then, yes, you are a saint.

*If you can't hold children in your arms, please hold
them in your heart.*

— CLARA MCBRIDE HALE

As she nears the mall entrance, Jocelyn
recognizes eleven-year-old Tom from the after-
school program she coordinates.

"Put your shirt on," his mom is saying. "The sign
says, 'No shirt, no shoes, no shopping,' so put it on!"

Tom, in one defiant move, pulls the shirt over
his head, stretches it down over his jeans.
"Satisfied?" he asks, dodging his mom's attempt
to hug him.

Jocelyn chooses another door to enter, smiling
to herself. She watches how Tom figures out some
okay way to make contact—just the way he does
with her at school.

He stands close to his mom so his arm touches
hers, or he paces himself so that he's walking at the
same speed she is. Jocelyn makes a mental note to
share her observations with Tom's mom when she
sees her again so she'll know Tom is still her boy,
depending on that place in her heart where only
he fits.

**Kids know you understand that their need to grow
doesn't mean they've outgrown their need for love.**

Truth burns up error.

— SOJOURNER TRUTH

On Monday morning, Jon's mom talked to Mari. "Jon's dad was supposed to take him fishing this weekend but he never showed up," she told Mari. "I'm afraid you might have a rough day."

When Jon's friend Monroe said that he went swimming with his family, Jon said, "That's nothing. My dad and I flew to Florida and went deep sea fishing. I caught a shark."

"Liar," Monroe retorted.

Jon screamed, "Am not!" and punched Monroe, making his nose bleed.

Mari took care of Monroe's nose and hurt feelings. Then she talked to Jon.

"Your mom told me your dad didn't visit," Mari said.

"Did too. We went fishing. I swear."

"Jon, come here." Mari wrapped her arms around him. "My dad used to hit me. I didn't want anybody to think he was mean. So I used to lie. I'm really sorry you feel so bad. Let's go do something nice for Monroe, okay?"

"Okay," said Jon, smearing his tears with his shirt sleeve.

Your loving compassion brings truth and love to problems that little children shouldn't have to face.

Never give up on a child.

— PATRICIA WILLIS

"Mikey's a baby. Mikey's a baby," the preschoolers chant when Mikey, the youngest, misuses the words "I" and "me."

"Me not a baby," he screams, jumping and stomping in a circle. The kids laugh and goad him on. Jan calls a halt to the scene, gets a kickball game started, and takes Mikey aside to the snack table.

"You say, 'I am not a baby,' not 'Me not a baby,'" she says. "When you ask for something, like this juice, say, 'I want some juice, please.' Say 'I.' Not 'me.'"

"Me don't like you," Mikey says defiantly.

"Well, I like you," Jan says. Laughing, she tousles his curls, gives him some juice, and moves toward the kickball game. Mikey gulps the drink and shouts, "Teacher, wait for I!"

Because you don't give up on kids, they don't give up on themselves. You've earned the endearing moments when they hurry to follow where your heart leads them.

Laughter brings us closer to the real us—the lovable us, the happy us, the free us, the us others want to be around.

— TERRY LYNN TAYLOR

Shannon, the after-school teacher, shoots baskets, plays outfield, and ties fishing flies with the kids. She makes them laugh and is their listening friend. One day, she is putting away the equipment and hears three girls, huddled in the corner of the yard, talking in their "I'm your best friend. Don't tell anyone" voices.

"I'm going to be a tattoo artist someday, for real. My parents will just flip," says Anastasia.

"I'll probably have three kids or something boring," sighs Gretal.

Leaning against the tree, Brook says matter-of-factly, "I'm not going to be a grown-up. I'm going to be like Shannon."

The free you, the lovable you, the one that kids like to be around, takes real joy in knowing that you are appreciated.

When there is room in the heart, there is room in the house.

— DANISH PROVERB

With the ten o'clock news over, Ron and Gail get ready to call it a day. When Ron checks the front door, he sees Delores coming up the walk carrying nine-month-old Tammy, one of their daytime charges. Delores usually brings her in the morning and Irv, her husband, picks her up at 5:30 each day.

Ron opens the door. Delores quickens her steps, stopping short of going into the house. She holds Tammy out, saying, "Will you keep her for tonight?"

Ron says, "What's the problem? Come in."

"I'd rather not. Won't you just take her?"

"Please, come in," Ron says.

The hall light falls on Delores's swollen face, discolored eye, and split lip.

Ron takes Tammy while Gail puts her arm around Delores's shoulder and asks, "Who did this?"

"Irv," she whispers. "Please, you do have room for Tammy?"

When you open your door to families, you open your heart to their joys and sorrows, showing the world how to care.

I used to want the words "She tried" on my tombstone.
Now I want "She did it."

— KATHERINE DUNHAM

The celebration over, orange, green, and black balloons hang limply from the pillars. But our spirits soar high and bright. We are a small group of teachers and parents who wrote grants, hammered nails, talked to corporations, and poured cement. People said we wouldn't be able to pull it off and build this center in our community for our kids. This building is now a place children will come to to learn about their heritage, to be proud and competent.

At today's opening, a parent thanked us. "If nothing else ever happened in this school," she said, "the fact that you did it is an inspiration forever."

You work hard for children. Congratulations for your creativity, courage, and perseverance.

Doorbells are like a magic game, or the grab bag at
a fair. You never know . . . who may be waiting there.

— RACHEL FIELD

From her child care home, Lila pulls two one
year olds in a farm style-coaster wagon, down a
quiet suburban street. Jennifer, 4, and Tyrice, 3,
help to pull. Lila's son, Billy, rides ahead on his
Big Wheel.

They have been promised a special treat at a
house in the middle of the block. Billy pumps into
the driveway where he waits for the rest to catch
up. Then he and Jennifer, on tiptoe, eagerly reach
for the doorbell.

The door opens. A small shiny-furred, beige dog
with a cone-shaped birthday hat perched between
long ears appears to answer their ring. Kids shriek
with delight. The little shih-tzu's large eyes shine.
Her pom-pom tail beats the air.

Her owners, white-haired Carl and Liz, say,
"Surprise! Table's ready. Four candles are on Missy's
cake. Ice cream and hats for everybody."

**The effort you put into special joyful events gives kids
a lifetime treasury of memories to draw on.**

The moment of victory is much too short to live for that and nothing else.

— MARTINA NAVRATILOVA

The kids were all on the floor, rolling with laughter.

"What's the joke?" asked Bern's uncle Greg.

"Nothing really," I answered. "It's a game where they try to make each other laugh."

"Bern's told me about those stupid noncompetitive games," said Greg. "I want him to learn how to be a winner, to get ready for the real world."

"You know," I said, "they say that only 1 percent of us are what the world calls winners. I'm trying to help these kids learn how to enjoy being in the top 99 percent."

Everybody's a winner when you teach children to have fun, figure things out, and cooperate. The real world could use more of that!

Some days should never be recorded, repeated,
or remembered.

— SUSAN L. LENZKES

Lumpkin, the center's guinea pig, goes home with Martha, the director, for the weekend. Her six-year-old daughter, Becky, cares for him and keeps him safe from Tiger, the family cat. On Sunday, Martha treats her kids, Becky, Nat, and Keri, to a long-planned outing to see Oliver at a community theater two hours away.

Once there, the kids settle into their seats but begin to whisper together excitedly just as Act I begins. Martha asks what the problem is, and Becky says tearfully, "I think I forgot to close Lumpkin's cage. And Tiger's in the house."

Nat whispers, "What'll we do?"

Keri begins to sniffle. Martha says, "Shhh. I'll call Gladys, next door. She has a key. If she's not home, we'll leave."

The first act ends as Martha returns. "Lumpkin's alive and well," she whispers. The kids applaud softly. And Martha is so grateful for a neighbor willing to rescue a guinea pig cowering behind a refrigerator.

Appreciate your special ability to handle a profession where a guinea pig may be your take-home work, creating days you'd rather not remember.

Chances, changes are all that you have.

— TANITA TIKARAM

Paula propped Sadie, the gurgling six month old, up on the pillow pile. From that comfortable spot, Sadie usually watched the world contentedly. But today, she tried to crawl. The pillows were too soft. She flopped, tried again, flopped, and tried again.

"Come on, Sadie," Paula said, "let's move you to the carpet. It looks like today is your day to go for the gold!"

Every day, in a hundred ways, you give children the chances and changes they need to win at life.

The longer I live, the more I believe in the effects of birth order in our lives.

— Frances Weaver

"My, he's tall for seven," people say about Chris. His younger brother, Rick, is two inches shorter. His eight-year-old sister, Angie, is petite and pretty.

At the learning center Chris is a tease. He moves crayons just out of other kids' reach, hides the ball, and delays games. When Alice, the teacher, asks him to put a puzzle away, he looks around and says, "Why should I?"

The director talks with Chris's mom.

"My parents visited this weekend," his mom says. "He was so bad that they couldn't get pictures of the kids. They told Chris to stand in the center behind the other two, because he's the tallest. He threw tantrums, sulked, and clowned. He ruined every shot."

The director says, "Maybe he's sending a message. He's not too-tall Chris—forever in the middle—he's a bright seven year old, wanting his own space."

You rescue kids when you recognize that what others label bad behavior is really a plea for love and understanding.

We cannot pretend to work for the best interests of children while ignoring the needs of their parents.

— JOYCE L. FRETT

Four-year-old Luelle swore at me again today. On her good days, she's a whiz at learning colors and shapes. The problem is that most days are angry days. Her mom takes three buses to get Luelle to child care and herself to work. As she rushed in two minutes late to pick up her daughter, I asked to talk about Luelle.

"I suppose you're telling me that she can't come here any more," Luelle's mom said.

"No," I said, "I just wanted to talk."

"We both need help," she sighed. "My mom beat me all the time. I said I'd never do that. But I get so tired and scared."

"Luelle's lucky to have a mom who loves her so much," I answered. "Call me tomorrow. I know some other moms who want to help each other out so we're starting a support group. You have a relaxing evening, now."

"I'll try. Thanks for talking."

When you pay attention to their parents' needs, you help nurture little children who come to you with generations of sorrow in their hearts.

Babies come into the world as love-dispensing and love-seeking beings.

— CHRISTINA BALDWIN

"Didn't think I'd be caring for kids again," Johanna tells the licensure worker. "But I figure long as I have my grandbaby here, I might as well help out other single moms."

"Infant care's hard to come by," the other woman answers. "I know. My Felicity tried. She couldn't find anybody she could afford."

"My mama used to always say babies were easy," Johanna remembers. "'Little ones, little worries,' she'd say, 'Big ones, big worries.' She was right. Babies ask for only what they're ready to give. And that's love. Lots of love."

You dispense love with every lullaby you hum, every bottle you hold, every hug you give—the world owes you much.

At work, you think of the children you have left at home. At home, you think of the work you've left unfinished. Such a struggle is unleashed within yourself. Your heart is rent.

— GOLDA MEIR

Here I am out in a grassy field doing the work that I am good at, that I love. I am caring for children.

We are all on our hands and knees looking for bugs and four-leaf clovers. What the kids can't tell, I hope, is that tears just welled up in my heart when I saw a mother walking her two laughing children through the park. I suddenly miss my own little ones. I know that my career is important, that my family needs the income. But today, at this moment, I want to be the mom with my laughing kids, walking through the park.

Being a working parent isn't easy. You give parents (and yourself, if you're a parent) permission to grieve the separations and celebrate work well done.

A word is dead, when it is said—some say. I say it just begins to live.

— EMILY DICKINSON

Every day Vernon's grandpa drives through the snarl of morning rush-hour traffic to bring Vernon to Sally's child care home.

Today Vernon's grandma brings him. "Grandpa's out of town," Vernon explains as Sally helps him out of his coat. "This is my grandma; she brought me today."

And with childish innocence, sparing not a single one of the expletives he had obviously overheard in the morning rush with grandpa, he adds, "And there weren't any @!!@!! stupid drivers today."

His embarrassed grandma says, "You mustn't swear!"

Three-year-old Lindsay, standing nearby, pipes, "That's right. Sally says we don't use square words here."

You have an awesome task when children look to you to help them understand the confusion of a world where words adults use, children mustn't say.

All you need in the world is love and laughter. That's all anybody needs. To have love in one hand and laughter in the other.

— AUGUST WILSON

The kids walked from place to place at the zoo, holding onto a yellow rope. They giggled at monkeys, laughed at clumsy bear cubs, and clapped when the seal balanced a ball on its nose. Two older women, who looked a lot like fairy godmothers, informally joined us.

"They are having more fun than our kids," I thought.

We ended the day with a picnic snack.

"Look!" squealed one of the children.

Over a little green hill appeared the two beaming women, carrying bouquets of red-and-blue balloons. We tied a balloon on each child's wrist. With their other hand, they picked up the rope. Balloons bobbing and faces grinning, the kids trotted to the school bus.

"Stay happy," their new friends sang out, waving their magic good-byes.

You hold out hands full of love to children and they hand you their world of simple beauty and laughter. Then everybody has all that they need.

Blessed is the influence of one true, loving, human soul on another.

— GEORGE ELIOT

Craig and Molly are looking for child care for Susie, their three-week-old daughter. They visit Delores's home, and she shows them around. Molly is nervous and polite. Craig's questions about Delores's experience and credentials are sharply worded, almost rude.

Molly apologizes. "It's hard for Craig to trust other people with Susie," she says.

Delores replies, "I understand. You have my references and referral from Child Care Resources. I like taking care of babies and have an opening now. You decide, and call me."

They call and Craig brings Susie every day. After six months, Delores tells him she is moving, but she will continue child care. However, her location won't be as convenient for him.

"Adds about half hour of driving time," Craig says in his crisp style. "Let you know tomorrow."

Next day he announces with a grin, "Susie says you're the only person for her. Her mom agrees. And I say you're worth any extra driving I might have to do."

You add a new dimension to their world when you build trust with those who find it hard to believe in people.

We don't have to give birth to children to know we are mothers of the world.

— MARIANNE WILLIAMSON

Five days a week, I take care of Jamie along with four other kids. I worry about his rashes and rock him when he's fussy. I was there to cheer him when he took his first steps. Yesterday when Jamie's mother came to pick him up, I was putting a bandage on a sidewalk scrape. Jamie was crying softly.

His mother swooped Jamie up and said, "How can you just listen to him cry? I can tell you've never been a parent!"

Sharing the parenting role isn't easy. When thoughtless comments question your credibility, let the love between you and the children be your strength.

Work all day, up all night, by morning nothing's going right.

— Venezuelan poem

Miriam does infant home care. Carrie, distraught, has come to see her about caring for five-month-old Nicole. "She's worn out Jeff, me, and a grandmother," she says.

Nicole, who wakes repeatedly at night, is a Korean child who has been with her adopted parents three months. Carrie looks exhausted, but her maternity leave is over; she has to go back to work.

"She wants to play. It doesn't matter that it's 1, 2, or 4 a.m. She's wonderful, but such a naughty baby," Carrie sighs.

Taking Nicole, Miriam murmurs to her, "We'll see if we can help get you on schedule. Mommy knows you're not naughty, just eager to get on with life."

The care you give and the experience you share not only comforts small ones, but also good people who look for support in parenting.

Sunday is sort of like a piece of bright gold brocade lying in a pile of white muslin weekdays.

— Yoshiko Uchida

"Oh, good," I thought when the morning sun slanted through the bedroom blinds. "It's still the weekend. I can work on that pile of receipts and make out the weekly lesson plans."

I took another five-minute snuggle into the covers. At my window, a pigeon cooed. The traffic hummed rather than rushed. My cat landed in a nest in the comforter and purred. In the morning calm I could hear my six year old sing to herself, "Today is a Mommy day, a Mommy day, a Mommy day."

"Come to think of it," I mused, "homemade blueberry muffins and a walk in the park sound perfect."

You know that life isn't all about what you do for a living, no matter how important it is. So you remember to give yourself bright, beautiful gift days.

Sometimes the desire to grow makes us feel "too little" when we are just the right size for now.

— LINDA CHING SLEDGE

"When will I be big enough to play basketball like Natalie?" Bessie asks her preschool teacher. Luann, busy setting out art supplies, answers, "Your sister is twelve. You'll have to grow quite a bit."

"How long will that take?" Bessie asks.

"Oh, several years," Luann replies.

"What am I supposed to do until then, always be too little?" Bessie persists.

As she turned to answer again, a small case of brushes slips from Luann's hand down between the supply cabinet and the wall. She struggles, first with a pencil, then with a ruler, trying unsuccessfully to pull the case toward her. She says, "Oh, I wish my hand was small enough."

Bessie scurries around her, gets down on her hands and knees, reaches in, and comes up smiling triumphantly with the case in her hand.

"See," Luann says, "You're just the right size."

When you show kids how to appreciate their unique talents, you help establish the self-esteem they'll need in the "big" world they're so eager to join.

A hundred years from now it will not matter what my bank account was, the sort of house I lived in, or the kind of car I drove, but the world might be different because I was important in the life of a child.

— ANONYMOUS

I stood in line at the bank, wondering if the fast food worker ahead of me was depositing a check bigger than mine, when someone tapped me on the shoulder.

"Hi, remember me?"

I remembered a sad little girl whose mother denied the father's abuse. I supported her mom and worked with counselors. One morning she and her mom just didn't show up. Now here she was, years later, carrying a briefcase.

"I certainly do. How are you?"

"Great. I'm a social worker."

"How's your mom?"

"She's fine. She lives out east."

She paused and then said quietly, "It's still hard for me to talk about those bad days. But me and mom prayed for you every night. She said you loved us into freedom. Thanks doesn't say it, but thanks."

Because you are important in the lives of many children, the world is a different place. Thanks.

With every deed you are sowing a seed, though the harvest you may never see.

— ELLA WHEELER WILCOX

Peter, a pediatrician, Steve, an engineer, Liza, a sports coach, and Girard, a P.R. executive, meet to celebrate the opening of a state-of-the-art community center for kids in their old neighborhood. They worked hard raising funds for it, and they reminisce about when they were fifth graders spending after-school hours at the old center.

"Wouldn't these computers have been nice?" Peter says.

"Math would have been a lot easier, for sure," Steve remarks.

"Probably so," Liza says, "You kept getting all of us into trouble because you were 'gifted but careless,' according to the teacher. Remember him, the retired college prof, the one who told us we needed a catchy slogan to keep us on track, so he tacked up that sign, 'Accuracy Counts'?"

"I remember," Steve says. "We thought it was a joke then, but, you know, it stayed with me. I have it on my office wall."

Your caring deeds and encouraging words plant the seeds for a rich harvest ahead for tomorrow's adults and the world they'll live in.

We are tomorrow's past.

— MARY WEBB

The rainstorm stopped. The kids and I had been cooped up during two days of thunder and showers. I grabbed a handful of craft sticks and said, "Come on, we're going to have fun the old-fashioned way." Outside the air smelled heavy and lush. Barefooted, we splashed in puddles and let gooey grass squeeze through our toes as we floated sticks down the gutters.

Prancing in her wet feet, Ming said, "This is my very best remember day!"

Tomorrow, children will remember the lively, lush memories you helped create today.

Above all, let children know you love them,
no matter what.

— Angela Stewart

Ross, a bright boy of three, is a foster child the Jensen's hope to adopt. Shawn Jensen is a writer, and her husband, Peter, is an illustrator. They've been Ross's parents since he was two months old.

They work out of their home, and today Shawn's going out of town to see a client. Despite Peter's efforts to keep Ross busy fingerpainting he finds reasons to interrupt his mother's packing.

"Help with my picture, Mommy," he'll say, or "Look, my shoe's untied, and I've got paint on my fingers."

"Mommy's going to miss her plane if she doesn't hurry. Why don't you go to the bathroom and then we'll watch The Little Mermaid," Peter says.

Shawn, with minutes to spare, searches for the walking shoes she plans to wear. She recalls hearing the clothes chute open when Ross was in the bathroom, so she runs downstairs. She finds her shoes in the unwashed laundry but the laces are gone.

"I flushed them in the toilet," Ross tearfully admits.

The gift of patience you give says, "love no matter what" to children who rely on it.

Mental health, like dandruff, crops up when you least expect it.

— ROBIN WORTHINGTON

Heavy gray clouds brought rain. The kids' restless energy brought on a headache. The budget wasn't balancing and the grilled cheese sandwiches burned.

The phone rang. "Good afternoon," I answered, trying to sound like I meant it.

Gladys, Desden's grandmother, said, "Hi, we parents decided it would be a good idea if you and the assistants went out for Chinese food and a movie Friday on us. Think you can handle that?"

When headaches crop up and you think you can't handle it, remember those parents who know that you work hard, care much, and give you surprises that make your day.

Look up, laugh, love, and live.

— MARY MARTIN

The kids sit at the lunch table with their teacher, taking turns telling stories about make-believe animals. As their imaginations run wild about everything from dinosaurs to unicorns, the teacher begins to laugh and says, "I think you're pulling my leg."

All talking stops. Small heads bend, look under the table, and pop back up again. Almost in unison, puzzled, small voices say, "No one's pulling your leg, Teacher."

You're a special person who can teach children to laugh at themselves because you do it with love.

Love is something like the clouds that were in the sky
   before the sun came out.
You cannot touch the clouds, you know;
but you feel the rain and know
how glad the flowers and the thirsty earth are
   to have it after a hot day.
You cannot touch love either;
but you feel the sweetness that it pours on everything.

— ANNIE SULLIVAN

The world is thirsty for the kind of love and
care that you give children.

As you do your work today,
take note of the sweetness that you pour
   on children
and how glad they are to receive it.

Tonight, sit quietly for a few minutes
in a cool, relaxing place.
Let the children's love refresh you
and rest assured that for years to come
lives will bloom and love will grow because
   you cared today.

One can never consent to creep when one feels an impulse to soar.

— HELEN KELLER

Three-year-old Arianna stomps and screams in front of the swing set, insisting she can swing alone and as high as her five-year-old brother, Rob. Judith, her mom, tries coaxing her away to ride on her Big Wheel but Arianna resists.

Judith's neighbor offers to take Arianna into her yard to play with her little dog, and Arianna willingly goes. For a while, Arianna rolls on the lawn with the pup, squealing with delight. But then she begins asking, "Where are your swings?" and is soon crying to go home.

Judith apologizes to her neighbor who hugs Arianna, lifts her back over the fence, and says, "She just wants to try her wings. Isn't that right, little eagle?"

Your encouragement of their efforts to fly gives little fledglings the support they need to someday soar like eagles.

What can you do with each moment of your life?
Love until you've loved it away.

— BOB FRANKIE

Sun-golden wheat swished softly in the summer breeze as seven-year-old Andrew and I walked to the mailbox. This short daily trek was our special time. While my teenage son read to the younger children, Andrew and I had space to share conversations.

"Look, a dragonfly!" I said.

"Are you over twenty-five years old?" he asked, kicking up small dust storms with his feet.

"I sure am," I answered. "Do you want to guess how old I am?"

"No. Does anyone live to be a hundred?"

"Some people, but not a lot. Why?"

"Oh, I just want to stay in life. How does that fly hover in the air like that?"

Life is full of magical, questioning moments that children share with you because they trust that you will love them in your gentle, truthful way.

Life happens at the level of events not of words.

— ALFRED ADLER

Lucretia, a first grader, watches eagerly for Grandma from the after-school club window. When Grandma arrives, Lucretia rushes to the door. Holding it ajar with one hand, she beckons wildly with the other. Grandma hurries inside. Lucretia says, "I had the best day of my life!"

"Well," Grandma asks, "What made it so 'best'?"

"Minnie and Mickey had babies. Lots of them. They're about this big," Lucretia replies, holding up her index finger, pulling Grandma toward the play room.

Glancing down, Grandma says, "Quite small."

"One problem," Lucretia chatters on. "Too many pet gerbils. Teacher says we'll have to separate the male and female for a while."

Kids will always remember the excitement of birth, and under your guidance, they learn to appreciate the events of life as they experience them.

. . . if you haven't forgiven yourself something, how can you forgive others?

— DOLORES HUERTA

As Timmy got out of the sandbox, his squat legs caught the corner and he fell down. His square little chin hit the dirt and split open. After Fran cleared the blood, she knew that stitches were in order.

She met Timmy's mom at the emergency room. "I'm so sorry," Fran told Timmy's mother. "I feel terrible about this. You just get to work and then have to come here."

Timmy's mother handed Fran a tissue. "Fran, accidents happen," she said. "Timmy's a lucky guy to have you caring for him. Give yourself a break, huh?"

Your devoted attention to children doesn't mean that everything will go perfectly. Give yourself permission to be human—it's an important part of your job description.

There are times when encouragement means a lot, and a word is enough to convey it.

— GRACE STRICKER DAWSON

This is a happy day for Jordan. He's bringing three-year-old Jody and four-year-old Jimmy home from foster care. He's arranged for child care during the day while he works. The family has stopped by the resource agency so he can register for the next series of parenting classes in the early childhood program he's pursuing.

The kids run straight to the toy corner, and Jordan stops at the front desk to fill out registration forms.

"Never learned anything about raising kids in school," he says to Denise, the receptionist. "I'm sure working at it now."

"Don't feel embarrassed about asking questions. The child care teachers and providers will help with behavior problems or whatever," Denise says.

"Most of them say the more they teach, the more they learn," Denise tells Jordan, "so use them. And remember, you're not alone. Many people have never even been around small kids until they have their own."

Your love, patience, and the child-rearing knowledge you share with the inexperienced, give encouragement beyond what words can say.

Some day we will win a beautiful life, if not for ourselves, then for our children.

— NGUYEN THI BINH

Between June and October, Phan Lo opens his doors before dawn. The sleepy children arrive as the older family members prepare for a day of selling greens at the market and pulling weeds in the gardens.

Phan Lo greets the families saying, "Good morning. How many beautiful children we have today. We will love them well and teach them to cherish your work for them. See you soon."

Children feel secure when they grow up treasuring their families. Because of your thoughtful care, families will win a beautiful life for their children.

The dog was created especially for children . . . the god of frolic.

— Henry Ward Beecher

Josie, almost four years old, screams piercingly whenever she's feeling exuberant, swinging high, or playing a running game. The other kids in Vi's home care usually cover their ears until she stopps, but lately they ask, "Do we have to play with her? She hurts our ears."

Last week, Vi noticed Josie talking softly to the little dog next door when it came to the fence and barked. The barking puzzled Josie, so she asked the owner why the dog did that. The neighbor said, "She's saying she wants to come in and play with you."

Josie, who inserts a 'w' sound into words where they don't belong, said, "How can she pway? She's only a dwog."

Vi thought, "Maybe a little calming time with a dog is the answer." She asked her neighbor if her pet could visit occasionally. They arranged a twice-a-week schedule.

When Josie screams, the dog howls and cowers, so she's learning to control her high-pitched shrieks. She doesn't want to hurt the long, floppy ears of a friend who comes to play.

The solutions you create especially for children, when problems arise, deliver gentle messages young hearts understand.

The social life of a child starts when she is born.

— Susanna Millar

With a big cookie in each hand, Billy, nineteen months, waddles over to the new toddler, Amelia. While his mother and Geneva watch, Billy holds one of the cookies out for Amelia. She takes it and the two kids plop on the floor. Looking over the top of their cookies, they begin a babbling friendship.

"Billy is really great with other kids," Geneva says, "Especially for his age."

His mom nods her head. "I tell people all the time how you've helped him become such a sweetie. Have I told you lately that I love you?" she asks Geneva with a chuckle.

What you begin with a child lasts for a lifetime. Give yourself credit for what you do and know that you deserve thanks often.

*It never ceases to amaze me how they can make me
forget what was bothering me when I walk in the door.*

— SARAH PROSHER

"This morning, one of my kids came running
to me with a poem," Norma tells her date. "He said,
'This is for you.' Supposedly, he'd written it. Being
two years old, of course, he hadn't. The poem said,
'Teacher helps me learn lots of things, on her every
word I wait. I take home new ideas and fun. Yes,
I think she's great.'

"Suddenly, I forgot all about the guy in line at
the credit union yesterday who talked about his job
and asked what I did for a living. When I said I
teach preschool, he asked when I'd be able to teach
school-aged kids.

"I said toddlers are my favorite age. Then he said,
'You mean you don't want to be a real teacher?' I felt
so put down until I got to work today, and there
was Aaron with his poem."

**Little people know they can count on you to feel
their gratitude for the love and learning you add
to their lives.**

In the absence of the sacred, nothing is sacred—
everything is for sale.

— OREN LYONS

Chris told the kids that if they earned the money, they could go to the amusement park at the end of the summer.

"Let's sell stuff," said the ever-enthusiastic Michele. "We can make cards, cookies, and coloring books."

"Yeah," added Janelle. "And I can sell my icky little brother. Maybe I'll get a nickel."

Her brother, Ruelle, walked away sadly.

"Did you mean what you said about selling your brother?" Chris asked Janelle. "Would you really want him to be sold to someone? Serious, now."

"Guess not."

"Some things are too important to joke about— like taking love away from somebody. Can you think of something to make it better?"

"Yeah, I can."

"I thought you could."

You teach children what to value in life. From you they learn about loyalty and love. When you sow seeds of respect, children grow to be caring, concerned people.

Men who change diapers change the world.
— MEN IN CHILD CARE PROJECT

Steve volunteers with Head Start after morning classes. Today at lunch, his large frame spills over the small, sturdy chair, but the toddlers don't notice. He has served up soup, sandwiches, and Jell-O gelatin and is now helping little Booker handle his spoon.

At the door, Nat, who works at the center, ushers preschoolers in from the playground, and says, "Starting to rain out there."

"Yeah, look, I got wet," Alex exclaims.

"Not as wet as me," Doug chants, and the other ten or so kids join in with "Or me. Or me."

They noisily hang slightly damp sweaters and jackets in their kid-sized lockers, and Nat says, "Come on. Regroup. We have to go to the bathroom before lunch."

Steve's toddlers watch the action, and Booker says, "I have to go potty, too."

Steve lifts him out of his chair. "You're a little late, but let's go," he says, snatching the disposables on his way out.

Men who work in child care do the world a service by being there for kids and modeling male nurturing as a positive force in the development of children.

Beauty is not caused—it is.
　　　　　　— EMILY DICKINSON

Some days I have time to notice—time to be there. Yesterday was one of those days. Sitting in the green grass, the children listened to me tell a story about a funny little black kitty. They giggled when she got tied up in grandma's yarn and understood when she shivered in fear in a thunderstorm.

While I talked, I saw the children's shining skin, sparkling eyes, and sun-framed hair. I paused and felt myself wrapped up in the beauty of their goodness and trust.

You take time to treasure the beautiful moments that renew your belief in the value of your work and in the goodness of children.

Children are the connoisseurs. What's precious to them has no price–only value.

— BEL KAUFMAN

Eight-year-old Maurice arrives at the after-school club's Cub Scout meeting excited about a three-pound coffee tin he holds in his arms.

"Wait till you see what I've got!" he says, hurrying to an activity table where he lifts the plastic lid from the tin and spills out about fifty empty thread spools.

"These were my grandma's," he tells the den mother.

His mom, misty-eyed, explains that when her mother-in-law died, her husband's family told the grandchildren they could ask for one thing from their grandma's apartment.

"While some wanted things like the grandfather clock or the television set," she said, "Maurice tugged at my jacket and whispered, 'Could I have the thread spools?'"

"His grandma sewed a lot, and when she emptied a spool of thread, she'd save it. The grandchildren would build with those spools for hours. Maurice searched until he found them, while I hoped someone hadn't trashed them. To him they're priceless."

Children share their treasures with you, because they know you see their value.

I am committed to a one world community and my
work with children lives inside of that commitment.

— GEVONEE (GENE) FORD

The children who come to the center on the
university campus are from different countries
around the world. Many of their parents are
studying in the United States, leaving friends
and familiarity to be together.

"It's amazing," one parent tells Sarah, the toddler
teacher. "These kids do so well with so many
different backgrounds. You must have six different
languages in this room."

"My theory is that it works because there's one
language that none of the children know very well
yet," Sarah replies.

"What's that?"

"Prejudice."

You build communities that teach children to respect
and honor each others' similarities and differences.
Your commitment could help change the world.

To be successful, the first thing to do is fall in love with your work.

— SISTER MARY LAURETTA

Meg browses through the neighborhood garage sale. Though she's worked full-time all summer in the church child care center, she can't afford much. She checks out the sweaters, jackets, jeans, and books. Nothing appeals.

Turning to leave, she stoops to clear a small box from her path and shrieks, "Look at these neat cars. They hook and unhook. The engine's here. It's all here." She picks up one small car after the other of a smoothly finished, hand-carved, wooden train set.

"We can never find good wooden toys we can afford. This is wonderful! Only a dollar!" she says, her teenage enthusiasm raising. She bounces to where the cash box is, train set in hand, fumbles in her jeans for money, and bubbles, "These are so cool!"

"You must really like working with kids," one of the neighbor women says.

"Love it!" says Meg.

Your success is in the love you bring to your work where it touches young lives, giving part of you to their growth and achievement.

All art requires courage.
— ANN TUCKER

Ten hands swirl the white shaving cream around the table.

"I'm drawing the wind," announces Howag, dashing slanted bold strokes.

"Looks like scribbles to me," says Pete.

Howag hesitates for a moment and then smushes the cream into more wild patterns.

"Maybe you haven't seen the wind, then," she says.

The courage to believe in themselves and the opportunities to express their creativity are two of the many gifts you wisely give to the children in your care.

When one helps another, both are strong.

— GERMAN PROVERB

Teen-age parenting class ends and Paula and Jean get their kids from child care in the gym and return to the classroom to talk to the instructor. Paula tells three-year-old Andy to wait. "I'll be done in a minute," she says.

Jean puts twelve-month-old Willie on the floor and his diaper bag on a nearby chair. For a while Willie sits and watches Andy bounce a small rubber ball. Then, unnoticed by his mom, Willie crawls toward the diaper bag, reaches up, and pulls at the strap.

When the chair tips toward Willie, Andy moves quickly and catches the chair. Willie then takes off for the hall door and stairway.

Andy follows and manages to tug and pull Willie back into the classroom. He puts Willie on the floor near him and returns to bouncing the ball. When the ball slips away, Willie scurries after it on all fours, picks it up, and tosses it toward a surprised Andy. "Gee, thanks," Andy says, "I didn't think you could do that!"

Your caring skills teach kids to help each other and take pride in one another's strengths.

What its children become, that will the
community become.

— SUZANNE LA FOLLETTE

The locksmiths arrived, carrying large metal safety locks for the classroom doors. The drill noise grated the four year olds' ears.

Hands held tight against his head, Clark said, "Why are they doing that?"

"So that we can get out of the room but no one can get in," I said.

"Why?" he asked.

"People are afraid that someone might come in and maybe hurt you," I answered, thinking that telling kids the truth is important.

"I'm afraid, too. Jeremy's brother showed me his real gun. He said it's to kill the bad guys. Am I a bad guy?"

"No, Clark, you're not a bad guy."

Children look to you to make sense out of this world. You soothe their fears as you work to make children and their communities safer.

There's many a battle fought daily the world knows nothing about.

— PHOEBE CARY

Rhonda, who works with drug-addicted babies, speaks to a group of retirees on behalf of a community coalition for the prevention of drug use during pregnancies.

Her presentation is polished and professional until she talks about Samantha, child of a mother addicted to crack cocaine. At birth, the tiny baby, so small she fit into Rhonda's hand, screamed piteously for a drug fix. The emotions overcome Rhonda, and she pauses to regain her poise.

When she continues speaking, pictures of Samantha and her caregivers, soothing, rocking, pacing, hushing her cries, flash on the overhead screen. The talk ends with a photo of the little girl, now one year old, no longer screaming for drugs but yet dependent for survival on a world beyond the reach of her small arms.

Eyes moisten and checkbooks come out of even the most plea-resistant pockets, giving Rhonda one small victory and courage to go on to seek the next.

You are giving a gift of limitless value to kids when you reach out for them to a world that otherwise would be unaware of their needs.

No one is rich enough to do without a neighbor.

— DANISH PROVERB

The well-groomed neighborhood was quiet until we moved in and opened our new home for child care. Then Big Wheels roamed the sidewalk. The sounds of kids splashing in pools and playing rhythm instruments filled the air. I could feel the older neighbors watching and imagined they wished a retired bank president would have taken over the "Baxters' place."

One Sunday at church, I saw the woman across the street. She introduced me to her sister saying, "This is the lady who raises kids instead of grass. You should see the cute little ones. Everyone on the block has so much fun watching them."

Children are a gift to all of us. You open your door to them and you bring richness and joy to the community.

I always felt honored when a child would unconsciously call me grandma.

— SISTER REGINA FLYNN

"Where there are kids, there are grandma stories," a retired teacher, speaking on behalf of the Children's Home, tells the Foster Grandmas Club. "Those who haven't known loving grandmas often borrow stories to tell.

"The other day a foster grandma from a group like yours made cookies with some of our five and six year olds. She helped them roll out sugar cookie dough and cut and bake small stars. Then she dipped into a bowl of dough with a spoon. 'These are drop cookies that we don't roll out,' she said as she let the dough fall from the spoon onto the cookie sheet.

"Later, sharing their treats with the toddlers, six-year-old Crystal, an abandoned child from a shelter, informed them, 'These are called drop cookies, so when grandmas go to heaven they can drop them down to us.'"

Kids associate you with the kind of "grandma" love storytellers write about, ever constant and dependable.

*Our most memorable days are marked by an
absence of control.*

— PATRICIA SMITH

Juan stayed in touch with some of the kids that
he cared for over the years. He had taught them to
write their names, count, cut, and color. One day
he had lunch with Kirk, now twenty-six years old.

"Sometimes I wonder what you remember best
about Juan's child care," Juan said over coffee.

Kirk thought only for a brief second and
answered with the voice of someone savoring a
delicious memory. "The day we rolled down the
hills in the park and landed splat! in the puddles
at the bottom," he remembered. "We laughed until
our faces and bellies hurt. One of the top ten days
in my life, without a doubt."

You give children memorable days full of the joy
of being young and carefree that they can savor for
years to come.

The first problem for all of us, men and women, is not to learn, but to unlearn.

— GLORIA STEINEM

Nelson is ironing doll clothes, folding them neatly as a three year old can, when his seventeen-year-old brother, Max, comes to pick him up.

"Hey, fella," Max says, "You don't do ironing. That's girl's stuff." He swings him up and out of the housekeeping corner.

"But Mom told Daddy it's like cooking and dishes, an equal op-por-tu-ni-ty job," Nelson says, stumbling on the five-syllable word.

"Not while I'm around," Max says.

Katrina, the preschool teacher, intervenes. "Well, Max," she says, "here boys and girls share."

As they leave Nelson says, "I'm telling Mom when we get home."

When you help children resist limiting stereotypes, you teach them about peaceful social change in a world that struggles with the volatile issue of equality.

Designer clothes worn by children are like snowsuits worn by adults. Few can carry them off successfully.

— FRAN LEBOWITZ

It was one of those spongy summer days when the only rational thing to do was to pull out the hose and make rivers and dams in the sand. Licking our frozen juice bars, the six sandpile engineers and I admired our achievements.

When Gretal's mother, Julie, arrived, Gretal raced to her mom. "Come and see the biggest river ever made by kids!" she shouted.

Julie pulled back and said, "Don't get any closer with those filthy clothes!" She looked at me and said, "I paid $30 for that sunsuit. Don't you teach kids to value anything?"

That night I wrote a polite note to the parents. "I teach kids creativity, problem solving, and pride in their skills. Sometimes these values get a little messy. Please dress your kids for real success."

You know what is important for kids, and you continue to educate others about what it takes to have a successful childhood.

Imagination is the highest kite one can fly.

— LAUREN BACALL

The lesson was about courtesy and good manners. To end it, Rhonda leads the toddlers through their song, "Two little magic words open any door with ease. One little word is 'thanks.' The other little word is 'please.'"

Later, the group waits while Rhonda tries to open a cupboard to get art supplies. She turns the handle several times, tugging and pulling.

"I can't imagine why this door won't open. We'll have to get some help with it," she tells the kids.

"Teacher," little Kirsten asks, "Why don't you try the two magic words?"

You add magic to learning and imagination to living, making childhood the wonderful time it should be.

Over the years our bodies become walking
autobiographies, telling friends and strangers
alike of the minor and major stresses of our lives.

— MARILYN FERGUSON

The bus to take the kids to the roller-skating rink was late. Confined to the indoors by a rainstorm, the ten year olds got restless. David decided to pelt eraser bits at the girls. Linda, the supervisor, heard the commotion.

"Get into my office right now, young man."

David slouched his way into a chair and stared at Linda.

Linda didn't usually go on like this, but it had been a long week. She peppered her five-minute talk with words like "responsibility," "effort," and "cooperation." She ended asking, "Do you have anything to say?"

David looked at her quizzically and said, "How did you get those wrinkles?"

When stresses and strains try to get the better of you, your sense of humor can keep those wrinkles to a minimum.

It is not what we do but how much love we put into it.

— Mother Teresa

"Everything's fine," the doctor says, looking up from Jane's physical reports. "You say you're tired, but otherwise feel good. You'd probably be less tired if you didn't take care of kids."

"Well, child care's what I do. I like it," says Jane. "People who leave their kids with me are tired too."

"True, but you could be putting too much of yourself into this baby-sitting business," says the doctor.

"I don't baby-sit. I take care of children. It's my job. I have training. I live with regulations, taxes, low pay, lack of professional recognition," says Jane, rising from her chair and moving toward the door. "Maybe that's what makes me tired. But you know what? I love kids. I don't think I can give them too much of that."

When you point out the importance of your profession to people who choose not to recognize its worth, you chip away at society's indifference to the needs of children.

We build our temples for tomorrow, strong as we know how, and we stand on top of the mountain, free within ourselves.

— LANGSTON HUGHES

Carol keeps nudging staff to include more multicultural materials and activities. When she gets tired of being a bother to her coworkers, she wonders if it is worth it. Then yesterday she saw Rebecca, a beautiful little African-American girl, leave the reading circle. Rebecca has Down's syndrome, very little speech, and a short attention span. Rebecca got a book that had an African-American girl on the cover. She touched her own face and then stroked the cover. Carefully she turned each page saying, "Pretty, pretty, pretty."

You show children the beauty that is theirs so that they can stand proud and free today and throughout their tomorrows.

Learn to be wise, to be silent, and to listen.

— TEACHINGS OF WHITE EAGLE

Dan Stover's wife is a researcher working on her Ph.D. He is home with their two preschoolers, doing licensed child care.

Jimmy Whitefoot, almost four years old, is one of Dan's charges. Jimmy's mom has gone back to school for her M.A., hoping to return to teaching. Jimmy, a shy little boy, begins coming to Dan's at the start of fall quarter.

Within days, Jimmy's shyness wears off. He runs up the walk when his mom drops him off. About the fifth week, however, Jimmy begins to lose interest in games and projects and his mom has to walk him to the door each morning.

When Dan mentions to her that something seems wrong with Jimmy, she bursts into tears.

"I know; it's my fault," she sobs. "Home is not a good place now. His dad wants a divorce, and I don't. And I'm not handling this well. Poor Jimmy."

Your experience gives you the sensitivity and wisdom to recognize and reach out for a troubled child.

I will not be satisfied living my life simply for myself.
Other issues are much broader than my own little world.

— ANITA HILL

Colleen's mother calls her daughter long distance, expecting a long chat. "Isn't it enough that you manage other people's kids all day?" her mother asks sharply. "Why are you running off at night to some meeting?"

Colleen lives in a little Appalachian town. She cares for kids while their moms sew at a women's collective. The money they make selling their work provides some of the basics like food and shoes.

"If you knew the families, Mom, you'd understand," answers Colleen. "Do you know any places back home that might sell the quilts the moms make? You should see them, they're exquisite."

"I can check. Maybe then you'll stop wearing yourself out. I worry about you."

"I'm fine, really, Mom. These women take care of me too. Gotta go. Call you!"

Rarely is your work finished when the last child goes home. Your dedication continues in countless ways because you care for many little worlds besides your own.

I'm not a child. I call myself a boy.

— SWINBURNE

Jeremy, 10, and Robert, 5, are new to the city. With their parents, they've come to visit the after-school Discovery Club.

Robert's wire rims shield inquisitive eyes that look at every poster and glance into every doorway. When the family meets Sheila, the director, Robert makes the introductions.

"He's Jeremy," he says, nodding toward his brother. "He likes to be called Jerry. I'm Robert. I prefer Robert."

When their parents leave, Sheila gives the boys a tour, introducing them to staff as Jerry and Robert. Jeremy shows interest in an aquarium that some kids are tending, so Sheila leaves him there.

Robert goes on with her, pausing at the puzzle table. Marcy, the teacher working with the kids, asks, "Would you like to join? There's always room for one more child."

Robert says, "I call myself a boy."

Kids develop healthy self-esteem and pride in who they are when they have your understanding, love, and support.

Big doesn't necessarily mean better. Sunflowers aren't better than violets.

— EDNA FERBER

Patrice is a snuggly, round-faced four year old with a love of peanut butter and a hatred for spiders. I know a lot about Patrice because she has been coming to my house since she was six weeks old. Two weeks ago her mother announced that Patrice would be going to a child care center in September.

"It's time for her to learn something before she goes to school," her mother had said.

I wanted to scream, "Learn something? Where do you think she learned to walk, talk, sing songs, and be kind?" But I didn't. Instead I said I would miss her and that I know some people at the center and they run a good program.

Yesterday Patrice left. She gave me a present and said, "My heart is hurting. Can you make it better?"

"Sing our 'I Love You' song and soon it will be just fine sweetie, just fine."

There is no sense blaming the sunflowers because someone doesn't appreciate the violets. Sing your own song and you will be fine, just fine.

One good friend is not to be weighed against the jewels of all the earth.

— ROBERT SOUTH

They run from opposite directions toward each other across the campus lawn, gleefully shouting "Hi" in their little girl voices. Long, dark, shiny ponytails and beaded braids bounce as they move.

"Maria Lopez, come back," calls Maria's mother. Hardly able to stand still, Maria stops and waits for her friend, Lisa. The two hug, jump up and down, and hug again in reunion after a summer apart.

"Pretty," says Lisa, touching the sequined pink bow in Maria's hair.

"You look pretty too," says Maria.

Arms entwined, the little girls do a half hop-jump step, attempting to skip together toward the student union. They'll spend the next three hours there while their moms go to class—the start of another school year.

Kathy and Terry, two twenty-something women in charge of community college child care, watch from the doorway.

Kathy asks, "Remind you of anything?"

"Us, sixteen years ago," says Terry.

When you help kids know each other, you foster harmony, nourish friendships, and add immeasurable richness to the lives you touch.

Nobody who has not been in the interior of a family can say what the difficulties of any individual of the family may be.

— JANE AUSTEN

Everyone thought that Patsy was the spoiled one in her family of four children. At nine years old, she had an attitude, wore designer clothes, and talked back a lot. Lee, the after-school teacher, spoke to Patsy's mother, who said that Patsy's dad gave her whatever she wanted. Lee didn't think the problem was that simple. Sensing a deep sadness in Patsy, Lee met with the principal and social worker. They told her to relax, that Patsy was just daddy's princess.

At age eleven, Patsy swallowed lots of pills. In the note she left, she wrote, "I'm sorry, Dad, but I can't let you hurt me any more. Good-bye.

"Love, your little Patsy."

You know children and the serious difficulties they can have. You show courage when you trust your feelings and stand up for children even when others don't agree. Your wisdom and efforts could save lives.

The possible's slow fuse is lit by the imagination.

— EMILY DICKINSON

Four-year-old Mary Beth has brought her doctor's kit and is holding office hours in the playroom. Sandra, another four year old, in the role of mother, waits with her twin toddlers who protest, chanting, "We don't want shots."

The doctor enters, and Sandra explains she has her boys there for the newly discovered chicken pox vaccination the doctor called about. Sandra helps to push up the toddlers' shirt sleeves, and Doctor Mary Beth applies the toy syringe.

Afterward, Sandra says, "Now that wasn't so bad was it?"

"Yes, it was," Todd says, faking a cry. "It hoorted!"

Randy, too, begins to cry. Sandra says, "It's all over. Now you're stronger."

Randy sobs harder. The two girls believe his tears are real, so they begin to cry. Ceil, their child care mom, puts her snack tray down and passes reassuring hugs all around.

"Girls, the boys are just fine," she says. "They're just very good pretenders. You didn't hurt anyone, Mary Beth. You were a good doctor. For now, though, you're out to lunch."

Under your care, children develop imaginations that may someday lead them to making discoveries the world has yet to dream of.

The sad truth is that excellence makes people nervous.
— SHANA ALEXANDER

Sharon runs a preschool child care program in a public school building. All of the teachers in her program have college degrees and spend many extra hours planning, bargain shopping, and fund-raising. Their program was one of the first in the nation to be accredited.

One day in the teachers' lounge, Sharon prepared a fruit tray for a group of legislators who were coming for a tour. She overheard two elementary teachers talking. "Those day care kids are so nasty," one teacher said. "Mothers should stay home with their kids."

"What amazes me," said the other, "is that Sharon has a masters degree in education. Don't you think she'd want to get an important job?"

Your job is important and you do it excellently. Don't let others' lack of understanding make you nervous.

You never can tell when you do an act what the result will be.

— ELLA WHEELER

Mark's mom told Mark he was also going to school so that the three and a half year old wouldn't fuss when his older brother and sister got on the big orange bus without him. Mark's mom brings him to the care center; he's excited and ready. He has two pencils in his shirt pocket and *Yertle the Turtle* in his hand.

Seeing his expectations, the toddler teacher decides to make time during the day to coach him on handling the pencil safely. She even shows him how to print "M" for Mark—a huge, unsteady "M"—but "M," nonetheless. He knows the Seuss book almost well enough to recite it, so she lets him "read" to her toddler group. She's pleased, sure that he's one happy camper.

Mom arrives and asks, "How was school?" Mark replies, "Didn't learn to read! Didn't learn to write! Never comin' back!"

Because you know kids, you can remain confident in the decisions you make, despite unexpected reactions.

Some people come into our lives and quickly leave.
Others come into our lives and leave such an impression
that they stay with us for all time.

— DOCIA ZAVITKOVSKY

Clara took her daughter, Marlissa, out of a residential school when the staff shaved her head. They said it was the only way to keep African-American hair clean.

At the new school, Clara told Amber, the teacher, "If she gets real loud, you have to tie her arms to the chair. At the old place, they used ropes. You can see the scars. Now she can't settle down without ties."

Tears fell down Amber's face. "I'm sorry your daughter went through so much," she said.

"Don't let her get attached to you," cautioned Clara.

"Why not?" asked Amber.

"You're one of the nice ones," Clara replied. "They never last. I don't want her heart to get broken."

"Kindness never leaves us," Amber said.

Nodding in agreement, Clara patted Marlissa's hand. "You can trust this lady, honey," she told her daughter. "She's got a great, big, smart heart."

Your belief in children heals old hurts. Your love becomes part of their lives for all time.

To teach is to learn.

— JAPANESE PROVERB

Mary and Rose Marie, first-grade teachers, open the double doors to Kennedy Elementary School, headed for their first teaching jobs.

"My mother asked me what I thought was the most important thing I learned in college. I told her it was that I would never be able to begin to tap all there is in the world to learn," Mary says.

"That's what unnerves me," says Rose Marie. "There's so much stuff out there that affects kids that we don't know about."

"We'll have to give ourselves time," Mary says. "We'll be a big part of their world, and we'll learn from them about the other parts."

You are a major part of the world of kids, and of a network of people who mold the nation's future by nurturing its children.

The only good teachers for you are those friends who love you, who think you are interesting, or very important, or wonderfully funny.

— BRENDA UELAND

Sam cooed and blew tiny bubbles while Lecretia sang softly to him. Sometimes the room lit up when they exchanged smiles.

"Isn't he just gorgeous?" she asked me.

"Have you ever met a child you didn't think was beautiful and brilliant?" I asked in return.

"No," she answered quickly," I can't say I have."

In your loving care, all children grow up knowing that they are wonderful, interesting, funny people.

Love stretches your heart and makes you big inside.

— MARGARET WALKER

When two neighborhood preschoolers come by and ask to come in and play, Debbie, a college freshman supervising outdoor play for the kids in Riva's care, says, "Go ask your moms if it's okay. Then they'll know where you are."

"We can't. They went shopping and told us to stay here until they get back," they say.

"Are they going to come and get you?" Debbie asks.

"No, we'll go home when the noon whistle blows," they answer.

"These kids will be going in for lunch before that," Debbie says.

"That's okay. We'll play out here," they say.

At lunch Debbie angrily tells Riva about the kids. "Their moms know they can't just drop them off for free."

"Bad judgment on their part, Deb, and I'll call them," Riva says. "You took care of it like a pro by not letting the kids know how you felt. Good job!"

You are a caring person whom children badly need, but when unthinking people impose on your love for kids, let your head rule your expandable heart.

We must stand together; if we don't there will be no victory for any of us.

— MOTHER JONES

Family providers, center staff, and school district teachers came to receive training about art activities. Somehow a conversation about papier-mâché turned into a finger-pointing session.

Center folks didn't think homes did enough with the kids. Home providers thought the schools were heartless. The school staff said centers kept kids out of nursery school.

The instructor listened to the debates for a while. Finally she said, "Hold it. We're all in the business of caring about kids. Let's work together to do what's best for them."

We all want what's best for kids. When you tell others the importance of working as a team, you hasten victory for children and all who care for them.

I hear and I forget. I see and I remember. I do and I understand.

— CHINESE PROVERB

Charlie struggles to get all of his school stuff into his backpack. "Weren't you here when we had a session about how to do that?" the teacher asks.

"I was here, but I forgot," says the ten year old.

The teacher empties the backpack. "Watch. Put your books in like this," he says, demonstrating how to put the books in so their titles are visible.

"Now, try again," he tells Charlie.

Charlie slides in two spiral-backed notebooks, his grammar text and workbook, and a math book and stuffs in a snack. "It all fits," he grins.

At the after-school club, Charlie drops the backpack to the floor while he opens his locker. Nothing spills.

"See that," he says to his friend Kevin, who's scrambling after papers that slid out of his canvas pack. "Packed it myself."

Your patience with kids teaches not only the lesson at hand, but also gives kids the pride of accomplishment, so necessary for building faith in themselves.

Clear days feel so good and free
So light as a feather can be.

— FLORA PURIM

Fuzzy little rose-and-blue feathers and long, slender purple-and-yellow feathers lay on the white porcelain table. Children carefully choose feathers to glue onto the sun-splashed burlap, stretched between two pillars on the porch. Two children weave turquoise, gold, and lime yarn designs into the cloth. They all chat, create, and cooperate while I stand aside and let the bright, beautiful day happen.

You gently lead children to learn and live. Because of you, they will have many good memories of carefree childhood days.

Blessed are those who can give without remembering, and take without forgetting.

— ELIZABETH BIBESCO

Today the kids come, for the last time, to the Montessori school where Glenda works. The school policy had been to pay a standard living wage to all personnel and maintain a sliding fee scale for people who needed help. Financially, that's no longer possible so the school is closing.

Two-year-old Mandy's mom arrives and gives Glenda a letter she says is from Mandy. Glenda opens it warily, because this mom was never very friendly and complained easily. If Glenda would say, "Mandy had a happy day," her mom would answer, "She'd better be happy here. I pay enough."

The letter, however, reads, "I'll always love Glenda. She gave me hugs when I needed them. She read me books and sang songs with me and rubbed my back at naptime."

Added was a postscript from her mom, "When Mandy says her prayers each night, she always adds, 'And God bless Glenda too.' We'll miss you."

Savor the moments of gratitude; tuck them in your heart to draw on during long, dry periods when none come your way.

Solidarity builds heart. We need some way to be
brothers and sisters in this work. We need to bond.

— LINDA CRAWFORD

Once a month, the seven staff members go out for dinner. Every month on the way to the restaurant, one of them says, "Tonight is for fun. There'll be no shop talk."

"Right on!" everyone agrees.

Somehow, though, before the menu hits the table, they're talking about how sad Jorge is, Kelly's first step, the gifted picture Shawn drew, and Petri's biting. Every month after the last cup of coffee, someone says, "How did it get late so fast? All we talked about were the kids again."

Someone else says, "Next month is just for fun."

And everyone agrees.

You love your work and the children you do it for. You give and take heartful support when you share with others who understand.

Each child has its fairy godmother in its soul.

— PERCY BYSSHE SHELLEY

Mischa lives with his mom during the week and stays with his dad on weekends. On Friday night the six year old went to his dad's after a visit to the dentist, who removed a baby tooth that had refused to leave on its own. As usual, Mischa put the tooth under his pillow.

When his dad came in to say good night, Mischa showed him the vacant space in his mouth and the treasured tooth. In the morning, Mischa reached under his pillow and found a ten-dollar bill. "Wow!" he said. "The tooth fairy's never left me this much before."

"Maybe he didn't have change," his dad said.

"Cool! I'll buy a video for the after-school club with this. The kids'll think I'm better than any tooth fairy."

Much more than they believe in fairies, kids believe in you.

*My mom always said the quickest way not to get what
you want in the world is not to ask for it.*

— ANNA PEREZ

Three-year-old Steven, who usually talks a
mile a minute, points to the cupboard. Jolene, who
started to take care of him and his sister Annie two
weeks ago, doesn't notice. So Steven adds a whine
and points again.

Annie says, "Steven wants a cracker."

"How do you know that?" Jolene asks.

"I just know. My mom would know too."

"I see. It's very nice that you help your brother.
But you know what?"

"What?"

"He's getting to be a big boy now. Maybe we can
help him ask for things so when you're not around
he can get what he needs."

"Steven, say c-r-a-c-k-e-r," coaches Annie.

"Give me a cracker!" Steven shouts.

"I teached him," Annie grins.

You notice what lessons need to be taught. From you
kids learn many things, including voicing their needs to
get what they want in this world.

We must treat our children as potential academic superstars . . .

— CHRISTOPHER EDGE

Raul says he's going to be a scientist, so he brings his toy microscope, complete with a slide that has some "germs" on it, for the other preschoolers to see. He tells them these germs are the reason they have to wash their hands before they eat.

Impressed, the kids do an especially good job of hand washing before snack time. Afterward, as usual, they line up at the sink to rinse their plates and cups and put them in the dish drainer. The line moves along well until Raul's turn.

He takes already-rinsed dishes from the drainer and rinses them again, ignoring the kids behind him who object and tell him to "Hurry up." The teacher steps in and asks why he's redoing dishes.

In a half whisper, he tells her, "Germs are really micro-organisms. I have to be sure they got them all off."

Your encouragement of children's dreams promotes exploration and discovery—it is the launching pad of our potential superstars.

When children are born, they are free and should always be treated in the same way.

— ARTICLE I. *UNITED NATIONS UNIVERSAL DECLARATION OF HUMAN RIGHTS*

When eight-year-old Marlis comes home from school, she locks her door and pulls down the shades. She follows her mother's orders not to go outside or answer the door or the phone. When I asked her mother why Marlis no longer attends the after-school club, she said there wasn't enough for Marlis to do in the program and she was picking up bad language.

One day I met Marlis in the school cafeteria.

"How's it going being at home?"

"Don't tell anybody, promise," she whispers. "I'm scared and get really lonesome. But I can't tell my mom. It would make her sad. She can't afford to send me to club anymore. Since Dad left we don't even have enough money to rent a movie. Don't tell. Promise?"

Your work is a promise to children that you will keep trying to make things better for them so that they can grow in the sunshine of childhood freedom.

Creative minds have been known to survive any kind of bad training.

— ANNA FREUD

Mary Ellen, a high schooler, decides to volunteer twice a week at the community center Head Start program. On her first day the director tells her, "We try to take a positive approach with the children and avoid too many 'don'ts.' Instead of 'Don't leave the toy in the middle of the floor,' we say, 'Put the toy on the shelf, please.'"

At lunch, two children spill their juice on the floor. Mary Ellen is cleaning it up when three-year-old Jeanie approaches.

"Don't step in the juice," Mary Ellen says quickly. Then nervously she corrects her error and says, "Walk around the spill please, Jeanie."

Jeanie continues toward the puddle as though she's going right on through. As Mary Ellen scurries to stop her, Jeanie gingerly taps the toe of her shoe into and out of the juice and walks past it to her chair, grinning mischievously.

You may worry about the consequences of small mistakes you make, but kids survive them and get the message of love and care you intend.

There is a use for almost anything.

— George Washington Carver

As I counted out the stones for the egg carton counting game, I complained to no one in particular, "I'm really tired of using garbage to make toys. People should appreciate the fact that it takes money to give kids what they need."

Tiffany, 7, handed me a folded paper that night as she left. In large markered letters it said, "All we need is love. Thank you. Tif."

You deserve more for all that you do for children. Sometimes, though, there isn't anything more useful than their love.

Those who open their hearts to others...are the
wonderful, warmhearted people who make the
difference in our lives.

— D. MANNING

The streetlights sway in the night breeze, casting frightening shadows for Michelle who runs as fast as her legs will move.

"Don't be scared, Sissy," she says to the white-and-black kitten she carries.

She keeps her pace for four city blocks and stops at a red brick four-plex. She runs up two flights and rings the bell to Martha's apartment, a teacher in her after-school program.

Martha's husband, Norman, opens the door. "Who do we have here?" he says.

Behind him, Martha says, "Michelle! Come in."

"They're drunk, throwing things, yelling, and fighting. Pleas-s-se don't make Sissy and me go home," Michelle sobs. In another room, Norman makes a phone call, returns, car keys in hand, and quietly says, "I'll handle it."

Martha hears his car move away from the curb, as she softly says to the trembling child, "No, no, no. We'll keep you safe."

When you open your heart to children, problems sometimes walk in with them, like frightening shadows that only someone like you can chase away.

Remember what the dormouse said:
"Feed your head,
* Feed your head,*
* Feed your head."*

— GRACE WING SLICK

The day over, I sit on the sunset lit deck, studying the textbook for my Saturday Spanish class.

"I'll be quiet as a mouse," my daughter's little friend says, tiptoeing up the steps. "Your mom looks busy."

"After all the noise she hears all day," my wise offspring answers, "not even a brass band would bother her when she's got a good book."

You deserve to do what you enjoy doing. Besides, you know you're a better caregiver when you make the time to "feed your head."

Success is failure turned inside out.

— ANONYMOUS

Craig, a five year old, works at making a clay flower pot for his grandma. He tries working the clay evenly around a small wooden bowl for the shape he wants. He starts over several times and finally puts it down with a sigh.

Faye, his teacher, sees his frustration and asks, "Why don't you try this?" She reshapes the clay, shows him how to work the bowl into it, and moves on.

Craig tries what his teacher suggests. "Like this," he says to himself, twisting and turning the bowl. But he can't force the bowl into the clay for the deep pot he envisions. Disappointed, he puts his clay pot on the shelf and says, "Maybe it'll be okay for a tiny plant."

His grandma arrives and Faye reminds him, "Don't forget your surprise."

He returns with it, ready to explain the pot that failed. But his grandma exclaims, "Just what I need for my straight pins! How did you make it just right?"

Delighted, Craig says proudly, "Tomorrow I'll paint it for you."

Children's self-esteem blossoms under your guidance because you know how to let them create their own success.

When you make the world tolerable for yourself, you make it tolerable for others.

— ANAÏS NIN

Gena's mom showed up a little too early last week, or maybe it was just the right time.

I felt lousy all week. Not sick enough to be in bed, just that hot and cold nauseous thing. The kids seemed to be crying and saying "no" much more often than usual. I went through the motions of art, stories, and songs until Kami spit her juice all over the table. I raised my voice. I said things that I didn't mean. My eyes filled with hot tears when I noticed Gena's mom.

"I'll clean this up," she said. "You look terrible. You know, indispensable taken-for-granted people get sick too."

You don't have to ask yourself to be superhuman. You have the right to take care of yourself—to make life tolerable for you and the children.

Keep within your heart a place apart where little dreams may go.

— LOUISE DRISCOLL

Caron, with her one-year-old son Reggie, moved from the West Coast to a midwestern state. New at parenting and frightened about leaving Reggie, she nervously reads the names on a child care referral list and selects a home care provider whom she can get to by bus. At 2 p.m. Saturday, with Reggie in her arms, she rings the bell at Annie Bexter's house.

"Come in," Annie says warmly, thus beginning a parent-provider relationship that Caron calls "a dream come true." In two years, Caron, Annie, and Reggie together have come through measles, chicken pox, colds, flu, and behavioral problems. Last week when Caron lost her job, Annie said she would take Reggie on a drop-in basis until Caron found work, and she'd keep a slot open for him.

"But you'll lose money," Caron said.

Taking her hand, Annie replied, "Sometimes there's a place where no one else fits."

Your compassionate heart and spirit keep dreams alive for children and their families.

Funding and resources should be equal to the needs that children face.

— JONATHON KOZOL

Families need child care but can't pay the whole cost. Our staff helps pick up the slack. We work at salaries that qualify us for food stamps. We make toys out of others' junk. So when a child care group invited us to a rally, saying, "Bring the kids and ask officials for funding," we went.

On a crunchy fall day preschoolers and staff boarded the city bus. Downtown workers grumbled as the kids' small steps slowed down the fast lane. When our commissioner invited us to his mahogany office, some kids pressed their noses against the twenty-first story window. Rachel, much to the official's horror, leapt into the leather chair.

Spinning around she asked, "Do we get our money now? We need a swing set. And don't you think teacher could use some new clothes?"

You teach children to take small steps for justice. Maybe someday Rachel will sit in her own big chair and help get equity for children and their caregivers.

To children, childhood holds no particular advantage.

— KATHLEEN NORRIS

The soup is chicken noodle and the four kids at the table are spoon-to-mouth busy with lunch. One is three years old, the others five years old—in total, eighteen years of living among them—and the conversation between spoonfuls tells a lot about children and life.

"My dad threw a hairbrush at my mom last night," says Jenny.

"Did it hurt her?" asks Patrick.

"No. Mommy ducked. It hit the door," says Jenny.

"Well, I don't see my dad anymore cause he doesn't pay child support. You know, he could go to jail," says not-to-be-outdone Patrick.

"Wow!" the kids say, and the chatting stops. Only the click of spoons on bowls breaks the silence.

When you can't correct what's wrong for children, take comfort in knowing you're giving them a piece of childhood they may not otherwise have—safety and love.

Each time we fit things together we are creating—
whether it is to make a loaf of bread, a child, a day.

— CORITA KING

Eighteen-month-old Calvin takes the little plastic people out of their barns, houses, and gas stations. He fits them into any space he finds. I was getting tired of finding them in keyholes, heat registers, and cracks in doors, until one day when I saw him diligently putting the farmer into the space between the wall and the window seat. He twisted and turned the little person tightly into the space. Then he crawled down, stood back, and with a contented deep sigh said, "Good."

You respect the way children fit things together to make sense of their world. Your understanding creates a safe and loving place for them to be.

We find at the end of a perfect day the soul of a friend we've made.

— CARRIE JACOBS BOND

Richard, a kindergartner, refuses the bus to the after-school program. Big brother Russ walks him from school to the center each day.

"How can I keep my friends?" Richard asks Kate, the after-school teacher.

"What do you mean?" Kate asks.

"Well, Russ says he's my best friend. But now he likes a girl."

"Russ will always be your friend," Kate assures him. "You just need to like his new friend too."

"Not a girl," Richard says.

Kate selects two monitors to put away drawing supplies this week: Rebecca and Richard.

At the end of the week, when his mom comes for him, Richard tells her, "Tomorrow I take the bus."

"Really?" his mom asks.

"Rebecca takes the bus," the teacher explains.

"Russ won't have to walk with me anymore," says Richard.

He hugs Kate and whispers, "I hope Russ likes her."

You teach children valuable people skills as you guide them through new experiences toward friends to share them with.

You can't kill the spirit
It's like a mountain old and strong;
it lives on and on.

— NAOMI LITTLE BEAR

Donna and her family live in the mountains. In the spring little pink, purple, and yellow petaled flowers grace the hillsides. When her daughter was born, Donna named her Rose, one of the mountains' new life colors. When Rose was six weeks old, Donna returned to work and left her with Bea, her great aunt. One day, five months later, Bea went to get Rose from her bed. Rose was dead.

They buried her with beloved and necessary objects for her journey: petals from flowers, tiny shoes, her blanket, and a picture of Aunt Bea. As Donna and Bea sat with the little body, Donna said, "The love you gave Rose will make her life beautiful forever."

Your tender caring graces children with beautiful days. Remember, in the very difficult times, that your strong love lives on and on.

I like my truth unbuttered.

— SHANA ALEXANDER

Dalina just graduated from college. Full of fresh ideas, she loved her new teaching job. "The kids are so cute and smart too," she told her friends and family.

Some of them also had complicated lives. Dalina noticed that two-year-old Erica often had red welts on her thighs. Other staff were afraid to believe the worst of such a nice family. Dalina went to the director.

"You know, we can't get all upset before we know for sure. When you get a little more experience you'll understand," the director said.

Dalina responded, "If you're telling me I'm too young to be competent, I don't think so. I'll have to report this one on my own."

You dare to take the risks that protect children. Kids can lead safer and happier lives because, when necessary, you have the courage to tell the truth.

Love doesn't make the world go 'round. Love is what makes the ride worth it.

— FRANKLIN P. JONES

On a crisp fall day a girl, about nine years old, rings the bell at Bridget Ryan's house. Bridget answers, expecting a request for a school fund-raising project. The girl says, "Remember me? I'm Kelly."

Bridget gasps, "How could I not remember you?"

She reaches for the girl's hug and lets the tears come. "You're so beautiful," she whispers to this child, who came to her care home just six weeks old. At age five, she left to live in another state.

From her car in the driveway, Kelly's mom sends kisses blowing in the wind toward her small daughter in the warm embrace of a woman with whom she shares the love of her child.

Unlike many jobs, the rewards in your work aren't in dollars earned but in knowing that your love makes a difference in people's lives.

There is more to life than increasing its speed.

— MAHATMA GANDHI

We lined up at the bakery counter. Today's walk followed the aroma of baking bread. Noses pressed against the case, each child carefully chose a bun. The small-town baker patiently let us point to one roll and then another. It took twenty minutes to get six treats.

"Today," the baker said, "the tasty buns are free to these fine children who know how to appreciate good things."

You move through your days on kids' time, letting children take in the sights, sounds, and smells that will be their fondest memories.

The little cares that fretted me—I lost them yesterday.

— LOUISE IMOGENE GUINEY

"Yesterday, I felt pretty low because of a three year old," Anita tells her family child care group meeting. "He was getting anxious because his father was very late and all the other kids had gone home. When his dad arrived, Dean ran to him to show him the picture he had drawn. And I gave him my weekly newsletter. 'Great,' he said to Dean. 'Get your coat.'

"Then, right in front of me, he threw the picture and my newsletter in the hall wastebasket. I was devastated.

"But I reminded myself not to sweat the small things, and having my newsletter land, unread, in the trash, was a small thing. Appreciating Dean and his drawings are big stuff. And that's what I'm about."

You let the world know you value your work each time you set aside personal feelings to make kids feel valued and appreciated.

To nourish children and raise them against odds is in anytime, anyplace, more valuable than to fix bolts in a car or design nuclear weapons.

— MARILYN FRENCH

My husband's tenth class reunion was a week away. I had done the wifely things of buying a smashing new outfit and trying to lose five pounds. I was looking forward to a weekend away.

One night Jim said to me, "Say, hon, I think I'll go to the old school bash by myself. You won't have much in common with those people. You know, they've all got pretty big jobs. If I'm going to get ahead, I really can't show up with a baby-sitter, can I?"

You have a really big job raising the world's future. Hold your head up high and demand the respect that your work deserves.

If our American way of life fails the child, it fails us all.
— PEARL S. BUCK

The couple stand nervously before the judge's bench in busy juvenile court. Through an interpreter, the man says, "In our country, our community disciplines our children. We school them in our ways. They know our rules and the punishment for breaking them.

"We are a farming people. Our families know how to work together. But our children have become Americans. They reject our ways and try to fit into America. They get in much trouble."

The court-appointed counselor looks at the couple's son, a nine year old who sits slumped in his chair, eyes downcast—a statistic—part of the 50 percent rise in juvenile crime among seven to ten year olds. "Child," the counselor thinks to himself, "you come from courageous people who came to a strange land to save their kids, only to lose them. We have to find a way to save you."

Your efforts in child care are crucial to saving the kids, whether you work with one, five, or fifty—you make a difference in how they shape their lives.

Your children need your presence more than
your presents.

— JESSE JACKSON

Miranda, eighteen months old, was munching on a graham cracker when her mother came.

"If we have the strength to get to the airport," said her mom, "we'll be in Hawaii next week. Two months of seventy-hour weeks really did me in. Thanks to you and baby-sitters, Miranda got fed and bathed at least."

She wiped the brown mush from Miranda's hands. "Come on, sweetie. Let's hit the beach," she said. "You do remember me, don't you, honey?" The doubtful tone in her voice made it hard to tell if she was kidding.

You are the stable presence in many children's lives. Your care gives children the essential life foundations of security and attention.

*In the titanic struggle to get ahead . . . children are
increasingly relegated to the margins of life.*
— Sylvia Ann Hewlett

Ava has been Jake's nanny since his parents
divorced six years ago. Today she drives a van full
of noisy kids home from Jake's soccer game to
celebrate his eighth birthday.

They all traipse in through the kitchen to the
family room where they're going to watch videos
until the pizza is ready.

"Wow! Nice house," Russell says. "Nice mom too,"
he adds.

"She's not my mom," says Jake.

"She's always at the games, so I thought she was,"
Russ says.

"It's her job," says Jake. "But she's cool."

"Presents on the counter from your mom, Jake,"
Ava says. "One from your dad too. Didn't you see
them when you came in?"

Looking away from her and his friends, Jeff says,
"I'm not opening them till they have time to give
'em to me." Turning to Ava he says, "When do you
think that will be?"

"Soon, Jake. Soon," she says.

**When you hurt for kids, remember that you give them
someone to hold onto in a society where their real
needs often don't count.**

My dream, my vision is that Hotep [House] will show,
through our love and through our culture, that we can
make a profound difference in the children. We hug and
hug and hug again.

— AZANIA LITTLE-BROWN

Children at Hotep House come from tough
situations. Many of them know abuse, addiction,
and painful poverty. The staff at Hotep teach
African-American children about peaceful things
such as their culture, warm hugs, and hot food.
They also help the parents by supporting them for
a long time after the kids leave the shelter. The
caregivers work hard, love much, and heal many
children's broken lives. They truly practice hotep,
which means peace, from Imohotep, an ancient
African genius known as the world's first
physician.

You respectfully and lovingly hold children in your
care and in your heart. You are a hugger, a healer,
a peace giver.

Babies are such a nice way to start people.

— DON HEROLD

Clarissa tucks baby Jim into the antique wicker baby carriage she treasures and takes her four home care kids for a walk. The carriage fits her neighborhood, with its large turn-of-the-century renovated houses.

Nearby, on a street where the city bus runs, merchants have converted abandoned stores into ice cream parlors, coffeehouses, bakeries, art galleries, and cottage-type industries.

The day is warm and sunny, so Clarissa's little group meets a number of people who frequent this unique part of town, with its slower pace reminiscent of a time gone by. To everyone that smiles their way, Beth Ann, 3, points to the carriage and says, "We've got a baby in there."

People stop, peek in at Jim, and say, "So, you do" or "How nice!" With each comment, four little faces glow with pride in this tiny person who puts fun in their lives just by being.

You launch happy beginnings for babies who add pleasure to the world with their timeless baby charm that blossoms under your loving care.

In the little world where children have their existence,
there is nothing so finely perceived and nothing so finely
felt as injustice.

— CHARLES DICKENS

The kids listen attentively while Carla reads the book about the homeless little boy and his grandpa who live in the airport.

"What did you think about that story?" Carla asks.

"It's not fair," declares Serena. "They should have a house too. Me and my grandpa have a house."

"I don't think it's fair, either," agrees Carla. "What can we do about it?"

"We could share. I'll bring pennies and nickels."

"Okay," says Carla. "Tomorrow I'll bring a jar for pennies and nickels."

"A sharing jar, that's fair," decides Serena.

Your respect for children's sensitivity makes their little worlds more secure. Because you encourage them to care, their big world will be more just.

The rewards are numerous if you're looking in the right places.

— LUAUN M. PROULX

A survey questionnaire seeking information from child care providers asks, "What makes you feel good about taking care of children?"

Smiles and hugs from little kids top the list for most caregivers. Others say requests for help with projects or games from after-school kids who think themselves too old for hugs. Many caregivers list words of appreciation from parents, such as, "You're doing a wonderful job."

One preschool teacher writes, "I have four year olds draw a picture of themselves at the beginning of the year. At the end of the year, I make the same request. The beginning-of-the-year drawings will show a small stick figure next to larger stick figures, usually Mom and Dad or one or the other.

"The end-of-the-year drawings omit the large figures and the smaller one is considerably bigger and on its own—kicking a ball, drawing a picture, or reading a book. The growth is always unbelievable and so rewarding."

The smiles and hugs you get, and the confidence you give, are tributes to your skills and love that strengthen young hearts and minds for lessons yet unlearned.

*I look in the mirror through the eyes of the child
that was me.*

— JUDY COLLINS

I get on an elevator that has mirrored walls.
I hate that! Voices from my childhood say:
"Your sister is the pretty one, huh?"
"You'll outgrow your baby fat someday."
"If you'd brush your hair it would get thick."
I step out of the elevator on the eighteenth
floor, certain that I am worthless. In the hall, the
chairperson of the Just For Kids committee stops
me. "Brilliant presentation last month," he says.
"You really made a case for the kids."
"Where were you when I was growing up?"
I wonder to myself.

**When children remember your voice it will tell them
that they are capable, worthwhile people and they will
be proud of what they see in the mirror.**

Sharing is something more demanding than giving.
— MARY CATHERINE BATESON

Shelley's mom sent the preschoolers a treat of orange-frosted, happy-faced cookies with chocolate eyes and smiles. Joyce, their teacher, carries the cookie tin while kids search out colorful leaves in the park.

"Treat time," Joyce says and spreads a blanket under a shade tree, handing the tin to Shelley. She gives a cookie to each toddler sitting in the semicircle, hands outstretched. Cassie's cookie slips from Shelley's hand. Cassie grabs for it but it flips away. Attempting to rescue it, she crushes it.

"No more cookies to give," says Shelley to a weeping Cassie, sitting on Joyce's lap. The kids munch their treats, except for Nickey. He whispers to Joey who whispers to Lucy who whispers to Shelley. When the whisper chain reaches Joyce, she smiles and nods approval.

Then, from Nickey to Joey and on down, hand-to-hand, through the small group to Cassie, comes half of Nickey's orange-frosted treat.

Let your generous heart bask in the warmth of those sweet moments when kids put into practice the sharing and caring values they learn from you.

If I fall seven times, I will stand up eight.

— JAPANESE PROVERB

I understand the kids that people complain about: kids who don't sit still, go from project to project, talk out of turn. I was one of those kids. I know how it feels to always be on time out, to be called "bad," to be lonely. Tomorrow night I will be honored as "Child Care Worker of the Year." The award says I am creative, energetic, and ambitious.

I hope that years of shame don't keep me from saying, "I accept this honor in the name of the wonderful, struggling children who, like me, have attention deficit hyperactivity disorder—ADHD."

You break the cycle of shame when you lovingly teach children to stand up after they've been put down. You deserve the "Child Caregiver of the Year" award!

We are always starting over.
— MARY ROSE O'REILLEY

"What a field day! Exhausting!" sighs Patrick, a first-term teacher. He sits on the hall floor, resting against the wall, while Ann, the center's director, helps with coats and caps.

Excited kids talk all at once. "We went to the orchard," pipes Gordy. "They have apples named after computers."

"He's talking about McIntoshes," says Patrick.

"They even had brown apples," says Laurie.

"She's talking about carameled apples," Patrick interjects.

"I asked the man why they hang the apples so high. They have to have ladders or ride in a bucket to get 'em," Marji says. "He said they grow that way, high up."

"She also pointed to a van Gogh at the art gallery and asked who painted it. Then, she asked 'Is it dry yet?'" laughed Patrick. "That was funny. We had a good time, but I'm so tired my hair hurts."

"Perk up, Pat," Ann says. "Tomorrow, you get to start over."

Congratulate yourself for making each day a new beginning for kids who explore their world with you.

Advice is what we ask for when we already know the answer but we wish we didn't.

— ERICA JONG

"I have a headache this big," Nina told Rahel as they watched the kids on the playground. Then she yelled, "Stop going up that slide backwards! Looks like I have to go over there. They're not going to listen."

Rahel watched as Nina pulled two kids by the arms to get them off the slide.

Nina came back, "Too bad you couldn't make it to the party last night. We had a few and watched the game. Got to bed a little late, but...sorry, looks like I have to go over there again."

Rahel put her hand on Nina's shoulder. " Can you take some advice?" she asked.

"From you, yeah."

"Let me go over there while you take a break."

"Sure, thanks."

"And, Nina, weekends are made for parties."

"You're right. Thanks again," Nina said, her face a little flushed. "I needed that."

You know that loving care for children is important every day, so sometimes you gather your courage and give some needed advice, even though it's not easy.

Tears are the safety valves of the heart when too much pressure is laid on.

— ALBERT SMITH

Andy, a second grader, sits on the steps outside Carrie's family child care home, head down and cap in his hand. Carrie steps out, puts her arm around him, and asks, "Something wrong?"

Tearfully, he blurts out his story, "Yesterday my teacher said we'd have a party for her birthday today. So my mom made a corsage out of flowers from our yard for a present. The teacher put it on in the middle of the party and made a fuss about it.

"Mitch and Carter called me 'teacher's pet,' tripped me in the bus line, and wouldn't sit with me," he sobs.

"You did a very nice thing they didn't think of and wish they had. That's why they're being mean," Carrie says gently.

Taking his hand, she pulls him to his feet. "Come on," she says. "The kids have been waiting for you to play ball. Mitch and Carter will come around because you're a good friend to have, and they know it."

As kids face life's early tough lessons, you give them a safe place for tears, a harbor of understanding, and strength to move on.

Two parents can't raise a child any more than one. You need a whole community—everybody—to raise a child.

— TONI MORRISON

Andy and Garrison munched on syrup-dripping waffles. Leaning his hand on his chin, Andy grumbled, "Boy, my mom and dad were crabby last night. I wanted to eat at the pizza shop but no, we don't have enough money. Dad went to his night job and Mom made me go to my room while she cleaned. What a drag."

"Could you help your mom next time so she would get done faster?" I asked.

Garrison had his own question. "You have a mom and a dad who both live with you?"

"Yeah."

"Weird. I don't think I could take that."

You are a vital part of the community that families need. You ease the stress in kid's lives by providing them with stability and a sympathetic ear.

Imagination is only intelligence having fun.

— GEORGE SCIALABBE

Five-year-old Wendell, making buzzing sounds, has awakened the other kids. The room where they are napping grows abuzz with a low hum as the other kids join Wendell's game. They clutch their hands in the air, laughing and saying, between buzzes, "I've got one," "I've got two," or "I caught a firefly."

Colleen, raising the shades in the darkened room asks, "What's going on?"

Wendell says, "We're pretending we're catching bugs and putting them in jars, so they don't bite us anymore."

Colleen tousles his hair and says, "Pretend bugs don't bite."

"Oh, yeah, they do. I've got zillions of mosquito bites," Wendell says, lifting his T-shirt and displaying a full-blown case of chicken pox.

Appreciate all the skills you have that get parents and kids calmly through childhood crises, which have little to do with fun or imagination.

I had a "real" job for seven months. My soul fell asleep.

— BARBRO HEDSTROM

"Whew, I made it," I groaned, tossing my jacket on the floor and dropping myself into my friendly, frayed easy chair. I pressed "play" on the answering machine but didn't even hear the messages the first time through. My head was too full of the day: the sub who didn't show up, the child abuse report I filed, the state grant that was denied, the parent who lost her job, the toddler who called me pretty.

So I hit the button again. "Hi, sweetie," my favorite uncle's voice said. "Just in town to change planes. Sorry I missed you. Your mom tells me you're doing day care. Cute, but when are you going to get a 'real' job?"

So you ask, "How real can a job get?" You know it's real when your soul feels wide awake and your heart feels proud caring for the promise of our future.

Have a heart that never hardens, a temper that never tires, and a touch that never hurts.

— CHARLES DICKENS

"Ple-e-e-ze," Tracy begs.

Repeatedly, she wanders away from the preschool playroom and attempts to coax her way into her brother Todd's group of fifth graders, who are building a spook house in the gym.

Todd keeps interrupting Jerry, his teacher, who has kids working on a science project at the opposite end of the gym. "Tracy's buggin' us," he says. Twice the teacher returns Tracy to the preschoolers.

When she runs off with the peanut shells, which were meant to make a crunchy sound like cockroaches underfoot, Jerry gets them back and sets up a Lego building block project for Tracy to work on until the house is done.

Occasionally the builders call across the gym, "Almost ready, Tracy." Finally Todd runs over, dancing with excitement. "Okay, Tracy, we're set," he says.

"No," she says. "I don't care about your dumb house."

"C'mon," he pleads, pulling at her hand.

Tracy says, "No! I'm doing this now."

The teacher shrugs his shoulders and says, "Sorry, guys. Guess you better invite somebody else."

OCTOBER 23

Take a bow for the many times you've handled a child's exasperating unpredictability with a calm, gentle touch.

You lose a lot of time hating people.

— MARIAN ANDERSON

Marshall and I played a board game. "It's not my day," I said after a bad roll of the dice.

"My dad knew dice. He gambled and always won," Marshall said.

"Is your dad gone?"

"Mom divorced him. He threw me and my brother against the wall but he played with me sometimes."

"So you're glad you're safe but you miss him?"

Marshall's eyes looked far away for a moment. Then, shrugging his shoulders he said, "Yeah. But you know, life is life! My turn. Maybe I'll get lucky this time."

You are the bridge that allows children to move from hate and fear to acceptance and hope. Your tender listening helps them heal.

We have not inherited the Earth from our ancestors.
We have only borrowed it from our children.

Once a week, the preschoolers take large
paper bags with them on a walk in the park. They
pick up papers and beverage cans people have
tossed away. Four-year-old Theresa's father says,
"I thought Theresa was watching too much
television when she started doing exactly what
that child does in the commercial about
conserving resources.

"If I run the water while I brush my teeth, she
turns the faucet off and says, 'You're wasting water.'
If I leave the hall light on, she flicks it off and says,
'You're wasting electricity.' If I open a pop can she
says, 'That goes into the recycle box, you know.'
When she told me about your day at the park,
I understood why she's so into that commercial.

"I commend you folks. You do quite a job with
these kids," he tells the center director. "They're out
to save the earth, and I guess we just better help."

**You give kids ownership of their world when you
teach them to plan for their tomorrow.**

I know I walk in and out of several worlds every day.

— JOY HARJO

Clarice is a Chinese-American child care provider. She lives in the city with her mother and two children, does diversity training in the suburbs, and is on the state Children's Coalition board. She has an opening for a toddler. A parent answered her ad and they had a lengthy phone conversation during which Clarice told the mom about her experience, training, and philosophy. They set up a time for an interview.

When Clarice opened the door, the parent looked at her and said, "Oh, I'm afraid this won't work. I want my child with a baby-sitter who speaks good English."

Clarice replied, "Oh, don't worry. I speak fluent English, Chinese, childrenese, and bureaucratese. However, you're right, there may be a problem because I'm not a baby-sitter."

You wear many hats and speak many languages, every day. Congratulate yourself often for your talents and versatility.

The dedicated life is the life worth living. You must give with your whole heart.

— ANNIE DILLARD

Unita has moved from her small two-bedroom home to a larger, five-bedroom house so she can make room for two children she intends to add to her adopted family of five. She's chosen them already, but she needs to find them. They're a brother and sister, children of a single mom addicted to crack cocaine.

Jaline, the younger of the two, was born a few weeks ago in the hospital where Unita is a nurse. Unita is worried about her survival.

She learns the children are with their mom in a house raided several times for drugs. After work she goes there, frightened but determined. She asks for the mom who simply hands her the baby and her one-year-old brother.

At home, Unita holds them close and rocks them through the night. In the morning she'll see the authorities and two little lives will begin anew.

Yours is one of the whole hearts that go out to children every day, all with the same dedication to making the lives of kids worth living.

Whatever we believe about ourselves and our ability comes true for us.

— Susan L. Taylor

"Don't take this wrong, hon, but why should they let you run their center? All you've done is take care of kids here," Akiko's husband said.

"I am taking it wrong, Pete," Akiko replied. "I thought you understood how complicated what I do is. Not to mention eight years of night classes to get my degree. I think I'm more than ready to be a director."

The phone rang and Pete retreated to the TV room, hoping Akiko's conversation would last long enough to help her forget about his insensitivity.

Beaming, Akiko stood in front of the Monday night game.

"Guess what? You're looking at the new director of ABC Child Care!"

"You're the perfect choice," he said. "Didn't I tell you that all along?"

You keep right on believing in your own competency and credentials and soon the world will believe in you too.

There does not have to be powerlessness. The power is within ourselves.

— FAYE WATTLETON

Jason races from the bus shouting to the teacher at the center door, "Hurry. Carrie's gonna kill people."

Sharon runs to the scene where six-year-old Carrie has five boys captive, hands on their heads, ducking her backpack, which she swings in a circular motion with surprising speed. Grabbing the flying denim sack in midair, Sharon asks, "Carrie, what are you doing?"

"Every day they pick on Jason, push and shove him, 'cause he's the smallest on the bus. We're fighting back!" Carrie says, eyes blazing as she tightens her hold on the pack strap.

"You kids go in," Sharon says to the five would-be victims. To Carrie she says, "The backpack, please."

Weeping, Carrie lets go. Inside Sharon finds an assortment of small rocks. Putting her arm around Carrie, she leads the little girl inside. "It's all right," Sharon tells her. "We'll take care of Jason."

You teach kids about the peaceable power within themselves as you guide them through conflicts and turn them away from the violence that comes from feeling powerless.

You light a spark sometimes that you don't know you lit.
— OPRAH WINFREY

According to the school psychologists, Shalina saw letters backward and distorted. "Dyslexia" they called it. Shalina called it "my problem."

"My problem," she would say, "is that I'm dumb."

For a year, Shalina and I spent after-school time, Saturday mornings, and vacation days drawing letters in sand, reading words while marching to music, singing syllables. We ended each session with a shout, "Wow, am I good!"

Shalina moved away, joining a treasured group of children that I love and wonder about. Years later, I received a card.

"I hope this reaches you," the card read. "I teach special needs kids, now. Every day we end class shouting, 'Wow, am I good!' Thanks, Shalina."

Because of your patience and care, you often light the spark that children need—"Wow, are you good!"

Feel the fear and do it anyway.
— SUSAN JEFFERS

The fall air is warm so the kids gather around Julia in the backyard for story hour. From her book cart she selects a number of books and decides on a Halloween story with ghosts prancing on the cover. When she opens it, three-year-old Jamie lowers her head and covers her ears.

"Don't you like this book, Jamie?" Julia asks.

Jamie shakes her head. Doesn't look up.

Julia asks Marcie, who helps her in the afternoon, to take over. "Jamie, would you help me put these other books away?" she says.

Jamie eagerly leaves the circle.

"What's wrong with the Halloween story?" Julia asks.

"It'll have fullabaloneys in it," Jamie says, busily stacking books.

"Who said?" asks Julia.

"Daddy," says Jamie. "I told him my sisters, Beth and Debby, said the noises outside last night are goblins that'll get me. Daddy said, 'There's no such thing as a goblin. They're fullabaloney.'"

You provide a safe place for kids when they're coping with fears that no one else takes seriously.

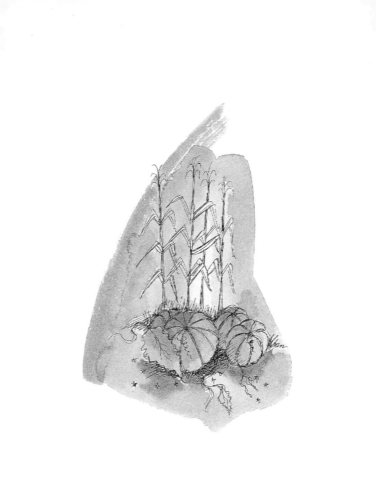

There are fairies at the bottom of our garden.

— ROSE FYLEMAN

Gingie, a fiery three-and-a-half-year-old redhead, tugs at her trike to get it over the threshold and into the house. Phyllis, the caregiver, who has Gingie for the day, gives the trike a final pull and closes the door

"Now you left little girl outside!" Gingie says, quickly reaching for the doorknob.

"Sorry, I didn't know she was here today," Phyllis says, reopening the door.

"She comes with me whenever I bring my trike," Gingie says.

"What's her name?" Phyllis asks.

"Mommy named her. She calls her 'imaginary.' But I just call her little girl."

At the open door, Gingie speaks soothingly, "You can come in."

She gets on her trike, backs it up, and says, "Get on. I'll give you a ride," and pedals off across the playroom. Looking back over her shoulder, she says, "Little girl says thank you for opening the door."

You give kids great joy because you let them step into a world where they always have friends—where fairies are possible at the bottom of a garden.

Poor people are allowed the same dreams as everyone else.

— KIMI GRAY

Byron is a teacher at a center in an affluent part of town. Teachers from other parts of town tell him about families who can't buy their kids shoes or pay for field trips because of the high cost of child care. Some of them are better off not working, so they give up and quit.

Byron decides to hand out flyers urging parents to write to legislators for more sliding fee money. One of the parents, who often thanks Byron for the fine job he does with the children, reads the flyer.

"You know," he comments to Byron, "I don't have too much sympathy for someone who can't make enough money in this day and age."

"I'm paid six dollars an hour. Is that enough?" Byron asks with a nervous laugh.

You are allowed to dream that someday you and all people who care for children will earn what they deserve. Working together, we can make our dreams come true.

There shouldn't be a single little child in America left alone to fend for himself [herself].

— MARY KEYSERLING

Irene Clark answers the soft knock at the front door. Seven-year-old Tommy, her new neighbor boy, says, "You take care of kids, don't you?"

"Well, yes, I do," says Irene. "Do you need something?"

"My mom's not home and I'm scared," he answers, chin quivering.

"Come in," Irene says. "You can stay here till your mom comes."

The phone rings. His mom is calling from work. "Tommy left a message on my voice mail that he was going to your house," she says. "I'm sorry about this. Could I talk to him?"

"Mom's really mad," Tommy says as he hangs up the phone. "I have to go."

"Wait just a minute." Irene says. "Here's my phone number. Your mom'll be home soon, but call me if you're scared."

On days you face limitations of what you can do for a child, realize that the concern you demonstrate can reverse bad judgments people make.

Peace is achieved one person at a time, through a series of friendships.

— FATMA REDA

"Hi, I'm Jackie Sota. You don't know me but Vera Forth said you might be able to help me."

"I'll try. Vera's helped me more than once."

"I have a four year old and a fifteen year old. They fight all the time. Vera said you know everything there is to know about kids. What can I do? I don't even want to come home at night because I feel like I'm entering a war zone."

It was naptime, so instead of getting my bookkeeping done, I pulled up a chair and listened.

At the end of our twenty-minute conversation, my friend's friend had pretty much figured out what she could do to help her situation. "Thanks," she said. "You sure do know what you're talking about. Have you ever thought of being a consultant for world peace?"

When you make the time to listen, to be a friend, you nudge the world to a more peaceful place.

Ask a lot, but take what is offered.

— RUSSIAN PROVERB

The kids select a theme for each month. Then they draw pictures to tell a story about it. In November they choose giving thanks.

After the teacher reads about the first Thanksgiving feast from a picture book, he asks the preschoolers, "In what month do we have a Thanksgiving feast?"

"October," four-year-old Marty quickly answers.

"No, November," the other kids shout in unison.

"I'm sticking to October," Marty says. "Jack-o-lanterns are easier to draw than turkeys."

Kids know you'll be proud of what they offer and delighted with the humor in the thoughts they express, giving them the confidence that comes with acceptance.

The only justification for ever looking down on somebody is to pick them up.

— JESSE L. JACKSON

Kalob arrives daily on "the short bus," as the other kids call the special education van. Kalob cruises through the door, driving his wheelchair like a motorcycle. In sign language, he asks, "Where's lunch?"

"Be patient, hungry guy," Melanie signs back.

Kalob doesn't have much patience, which is why there is usually a note from his school pinned to his shirt.

"This note is for me and your Mom. I guess I should read it."

"Go ahead," he signs, shining with a you're-in-for-a-surprise grin.

"Dear Melanie and Ms. Phillips," the note read. "Today Kalob taught me how to play wheelchair soccer. I missed the ball and fell out of my chair on my behind with both legs in the air. Kalob laughed only a little, helped me up, and told me, 'Melanie says practice makes perfect.' He is a good teacher. Sincerely, Georgia, phy ed instructor."

Kids really do pick up on what you tell them. From you they learn to look up to themselves and reach out a helping, respectful hand to others.

People are a part of their time. They are affected . . .
by the things that happen in their world.

— ELOISE GREENFIELD

"Because of AIDS, federal regulations may soon require gloves when we bottle-feed breast milk," the director tells staff. "Wonderful as it is that moms can express breast milk to us, milk is a body fluid."

Melinda from infant care objects. "We don't prop bottles because babies need hands-on touching and cuddling," she says. "Now we're supposed to limit the contact they need more of?"

"You hold them," the director says. "Your tenderness is there. I know you don't like it, but we need to protect ourselves, no different than dentists having to wear gloves."

"It's different," Melinda replies. "We wear gloves when we handle the milk to protect the babies, not us. When I hold a bottle for a baby and a tiny finger rests on mine, I think, 'This world needs you, honey. We're going to give you the best start we can.' A cold, synthetic touch doesn't send that message."

Your nurturing, cuddling, and cradling staves off the perils of the world for little ones and adds love to their time in it.

Let us practice the rituals of our families.

— YORUBA SAYING

"Teresa told me that you had weed soup for breakfast yesterday. I'm assuming it's another one of her stories," Teresa's mom, Opal, said.

"Actually, she was pretty close," I explained. "We had miso soup with rice. It had some seaweed in it."

"That sounds like a pretty gross breakfast to me," Opal said, screwing up her face.

"The kids went for it pretty well. Kinh's mom taught me how to make it. I try to put a touch of home into the kids' days here, you know."

"Sure, birthdays, security blankets, and grandparents' visits. But weed soup for breakfast?"

"Miso soup for breakfast, yep, sometimes. You better get going. You'll be late. See ya."

Because you honor all families, you weave a fine cloth of security and acceptance for the children in your care.

Work is either fun or drudgery. It depends on your attitude. I like fun.

— COLLEEN C. BARRETT

Dotty, a career executive from another state, is visiting her sister, June, who has a family of five and does family child care. At 7:30 a.m. the kids begin arriving. Three schoolagers have breakfast and go on to school with June's children. They all return for lunch, which Dotty insisted she could handle while June attends a parent conference.

She dons an apron and protective gloves, ladles soup, and serves crackers, sandwiches, and Jell-O gelatin salad. Though she works quickly, she's barely able to keep up with requests for "more please." Perspiration beads her forehead, as she clears the table and asks, "Who wants an ice cream bar?"

She puts one in each raised hand, while the kids giggle as though she's missed some joke. Collapsing onto a chair she asks, "What's so funny?"

June, who has returned unnoticed, laughs, "You just treated three neighbor kids to ice cream, twice. But, then, who's counting?"

Working with kids is challenging, and your ability to find fun in it teaches them the importance of attitude as they face the challenges of growing up.

Everyone can be great because everyone can serve.

— MARTIN LUTHER KING, JR.

Our special education class eagerly awaited the legislators' visit. When our guests arrived, Missi was serving "lunch" to her pals. A senator visited the make-believe restaurant.

"May I join you?" he asked in a sugary voice.

"Yes," said Missi, as she drove her wheelchair closer to get a good look.

"May I sit down and look at the menu?" The senator winked at the other adults, proud of his rapport with children.

"Actually," Missi announced, "my teacher says we should take turns. You can serve me, if you want." She handed the official an apron and order pad.

Somewhat surprised, he cleared his throat and said, "Of course, I'd love to serve you."

Missi pulled up to the table. "Then get started," she said.

Serving with a smile is a great thing to do. You do it every day and you do it very well.

Complacency is a far more dangerous attitude than outrage.

— NAOMI LITTLEBEAR

Louise, a volunteer lobbyist and fair-wage advocate for child care providers, drops off a stack of bright blue flyers at Carol's inner-city center. In bold letters, the flyers ask people to vote with children in mind, supporting candidates for office that support kids.

They list facts and figures about long waiting lists for Head Start and child care. They tell the numbers of kids home alone when school's out, and how many families struggle on poverty incomes or below, and the low pay for child care even in areas of affluence.

"They're great!" Carol says of the flyers. She puts them on a table near the door and reminds staff to hand them out. The end-of-day rush comes. Although lots of blue flyers go out, some people refuse them and say, "I don't vote. It doesn't change a thing."

In a world often too complacent to care, you are a beacon for children when you bravely express outrage in their behalf.

The great thing about getting older is that you don't lose all the other ages you've been.

— MADELEINE L'ENGLE

The workshop participants gave the instructor a long list of words describing the children they care for. Words like "aggressive," "selfish," "disrespectful," and "loud" peppered the list.

"Now I want you to go back to when you were the age of the children you take care of," she said.

As soothing music played, she asked, "What made you happy? What did you worry about? Who did you trust and why? Share with us, please, what you were like."

Timidly, words floated through the room: "scared," "insecure," "playful," "fragile."

"Tomorrow," she said, "let the kids know that their boisterous outside doesn't fool you. Tomorrow, find that love-seeking kid inside of each of them who is like you were, not that long ago."

When you remember what it was like to be the other ages you've been, you form relationships with children that are loving, respectful, and real.

Today a new sun rises for me; everything lives, everything is animated, . . . everything invites me to cherish it . . .

— ANNE DE LENCLOSE

Shirley hums as she paces back and forth, hushing four-month-old Melissa's cries. Her step is light as she moves to put the baby in her crib and she continues to softly sing, "You are the wind beneath my wings."

Edith, her volunteer aide, comments, "You're sure happy today."

"Yes, I am," Shirley says, "and you know why?" Not waiting for Edith's reply, she says, "Because this morning Toya's mother called, returning my call to her yesterday. I wanted to talk to her about moving Toya up to toddler care. She's eighteen months old now and handles life like a two year old.

"We talked about it a while, and then she said, 'What is your *professional* opinion?' That's the first time I've heard someone say that to me or to anyone else in child care, for that matter. I feel proud, and I feel good."

When the sunshine of acknowledgment shines on you, open your heart to its warmth—let it strengthen your soul.

I wiped my eyes and looked in the mirror. I was
surprised at what I saw . . . I was strong. I was pure.
I had genuine thoughts inside that no one could see,
that no one could ever take away from me.

— AMY TAN

As I closed the door behind Kora and her mother, Simone, I thought about the conversation we had just finished.

"It's hard for me to tell you this because Kora has been here since she was a baby," I said, " but I've taken a teaching job and won't be doing child care any more."

"What will I do?" Simone asked. "I've depended on you, and Kora loves you."

"Kora's ready to take a big step into the world. I'm sorry," I answered, tears pushing against my reassuring voice.

"No, I'm sorry," Simone corrected herself. "I'm being selfish. I knew you were too smart to be baby-sitting."

I glanced in the hall mirror. I wiped away the tear and let the hurt go.

See the genuine value of your work and know that you are strong.

Some people make the world more special just by being in it.

— ANONYMOUS

John is a fifth-grade teacher and athletic director, K–6. All the kids know him as a teacher who expects the best from them in the classroom and in the gym. He's also a proud father.

In the school library, between classes, he's squatting on his haunches, demonstrating to a colleague his small son's efforts to walk, when the door opens and a class files in.

He quickly unfolds his six-foot frame and straightens his tie, while the surprised kids wait. Feeling pretty silly, he hurries toward the door, lightly tapping his finger on the heads of a line of fourth graders who laugh with him as he leaves.

You make the world special for kids when you share with them your silly moments and let them laugh with you.

Where there is great love there are always miracles.
— WILLA CATHER

While their moms go to school or look for a job, the kids come to Home Away. At night they go back to the shelter.

Gus and his mom are homeless because Gus's dad beat him up in an alcoholic rage. He had abused Gus's mom many times, but the night it happened to her son she left.

Gus often hit other children, destroyed toys, and hurt himself. But he had a special attachment to Margy, the infant teacher. Sometimes she would let him watch her take care of the babies.

One day, Gus's preschool teacher overheard him in the housekeeping corner playing with the dolls. "Okay, cutie, let's get this diaper on," he said. "Why are you cryin'? Nobody hurts any babies around here. Nope, we just love 'em."

As painful as children's problems can sometimes be, your great love can help bring miracles into their lives.

Like as not, the child you can do the least with will be the one most likely to make you proud.

— MIGNON McLAUGHLIN

"Jude has become a five-year-old gang leader," Frances, a center teacher, tells Lorraine, the director. "He has groupies who mimic every disruptive thing he does."

Lorraine chats with Jude's father who says, "He's been impossible ever since we brought the baby home."

"So that's the problem. We'll see what we can do," Lorraine says.

Lorraine tells Frances to entice Jude's followers into some new activity when the misbehavior starts. That works, but Jude screams at her, "Stop that. They're mine!"

Lorraine intervenes, taking Jude to look at the ocean life book display in the science corner. Jude is fascinated and begins to study daily the pictures in the books. Soon he's drawing whales and identifying them in childish print.

Lorraine gives Jude's dad the drawings and tells him about an art program for gifted children. His dad eagerly takes the sample drawings and within a week an excited Jude begins attending classes.

How sweet it is when children gain from your wisdom and guidance. Share the pride when it happens.

Nothing in life is trivial. Life is whole wherever and whenever we touch it, and one moment or event is not more sacred than another.

— VIMALA THAKAR

Lia crawled toward the electrical outlet. We always covered outlets but somehow a cover was missing. I sprang up from the rocking chair where I had been reading to several children. Startled by my sudden leap across the room, they watched as I gathered Lia into my arms and held her up. "I love you, precious person," I said, and gave her five kisses. After I installed a new outlet cover, I returned to the reading group.

"Sorry I had to leave," I said.

"That's okay," Meleea said. "It was 'portant."

"It is important that we keep outlets safe, you're right."

"No," Meleea replied, with an impatient tone, "Kisses for baby's 'portant!"

You touch children's lives daily. Every moment that you tend lovingly to their needs is indeed important.

We are always the same age inside.

— GERTRUDE STEIN

Warren's uncle Jim is at the after-school club for Career Day. The ten to twelve year olds will make lunch. He unloads two large grocery bags and directs Gary, Irving, and Fred to wash lettuce and tomatoes. As he supervises Pauline toasting wheat bread, he tells a story.

"When I was twelve years old," he says, "I spent a day helping a favorite aunt. I hoed her garden and planted a willow tree. I worked hard.

"She made a lunch that made me feel like someone really special. She had clubhouse sandwiches, cut into fancy little triangles. Toothpicks held together the toast, red tomatoes, green lettuce, and turkey. The triangles surrounded chips in the center of a plate, with a pickle on the side.

"I never forgot feeling so special. Now I'm a chef. I've made hundreds of clubhouse sandwiches. I always try to make them like Aunt Jane's so others feel as special as I did when I was twelve years old."

You help kids build happy memories that will live with them no matter what life path they choose.

If you wait until you can afford to enjoy life, you might miss out on all the fun.

— DOROTHY SALONE

The family enjoyed the luxury of Saturday morning pancakes and reading the paper. No one had to rush and, best of all for eight-year-old Holly, none of "those kids" that her mom takes care of would be around.

"Oh, look at this," her mom said. "The children's theater is doing *The Cat in the Hat* next month. The tickets are a little steep but the kids love that story. I'm going to take them."

"I'll bet you mean 'those kids,' not 'your kids,'" Holly groaned.

"Yeah, honey, I do. It's during the school day. Sorry."

"It wouldn't help if you won the lottery. You'd give it all away," Holly complained.

"Just looking at you makes me feel like I have a million bucks. What if you take a day off school and come with us?" her mom asked, gently tickling Holly under the chin.

Participating in life, joining in the fun, and doing the unexpected doesn't have to be expensive. However you do it, you teach kids that life is an adventure to be shared.

There is nothing like a group of four year olds to bring one down to normal size.

— DOCIA ZAVITKOVSKY

Grace, a retired librarian, comes weekly to her daughter Josie's family child care home to read and tell stories to a group of four year olds.

Today she reads *The Little Engine that Could* and then tells about the traveling she has done by train through high mountains and many miles.

When the story is over, kids begin to ask questions all at once. Grace asks them to raise their hands, so they would each get a turn to talk. She calls on Leslie, who had listened intently, her eyes riveted on Grace all through the story. Leslie asks, "Do you know you have wrinkles?"

Surprised, Grace thinks quickly about how to stay on the topic of trains and travel. "Yes, but they're really adventure lines," she answers.

Then Jackie, sitting next to Leslie, pipes, "Maybe you shouldn't a'venture so much."

Your "You-gotta-love-'em" attitude is precious to kids because it allows them to learn by being openly curious and candid, which is natural to them.

I've learned only that you never say never.

— MARIANA VON NEUMANN WHITMAN

Lucia takes care of Miranda, Douglas's three year old. Lucia has five children of her own who are grown and, as she says, "almost civilized." One evening, Douglas talks to Lucia about his teenage niece who stays out too late and gets D's at school. "I'll tell you one thing," he declares. "Miranda will never get by with that. I won't stand for it!"

Lucia smiles and worries as she says, "Douglas, we can only do the best we can. One word I didn't use raising and helping raise a lot of kids is "never." We simply don't know."

You are a wisdom giver for parents, as well as children, even though you may never admit it.

I may not be making a living, but I'm making a difference.

— RACHEL HICKERSON

At 6 p.m. Maurie arrives home, gets her mail, and reads a notice that the rent is going up. She wonders how she'll make her money stretch.

At 6 a.m. she's off again to the community center. There she meets the Head Start bus from a homeless shelter, lifts babies from infant seats into waiting arms, and comforts Casey who's sobbing, "I want my mommy."

She settles him in with four year olds, then moves on to warm bottles, change diapers, rock babies, and hum lullabies. With the crib crowd content, she scrubs her hands and pulls on plastic gloves to serve snacks. After cleanup, she's down on the bright blue floor mat, encouraging infant attempts at mobility.

The bus returns. Casey shows her his drawing of a stick boy waving good-bye to his stick mom, both smiling. Maurie chuckles and collects her coat and purse. She heads home, where the rent goes up and $4.25 per hour refuses to stretch.

Though your compensation can never equal your worth, you make a big difference by giving children a good beginning and a chance for a promising life.

The nice thing about teamwork is that you always have others on your side.

— MARGARET CARTY

Julie, a college student, coaches third-grade girl's basketball. She teaches teamwork. In turn, she learns the joy of kids.

"It works better if you dribble the ball, not carry it," she tells one player. She chuckles, realizing how patient she is becoming.

"You're not tough enough so we're not winning enough games. We've decided to find another coach," a parent says.

Julie tells the team of the parents' decision and asks to meet with the parents the next day. Anxiously she walks into the gym. The girls are holding large signs saying, "We love Julie!" "Keep Julie!"

"Sorry," says one parent. "The team got together and convinced us that we forgot what's important. Will you consider staying?"

Children learn from you the skills that make them cooperative, loyal, and successful. Go team!

Perhaps too much of everything is as bad as too little.

— EDNA FERBER

Desiree's dad brings a change of clothes to Robin's family child care home in the morning for Desiree's afternoon kindergarten class. Lately Desiree has been unhappy with what she finds in her classy little garment bag.

"Not those socks with that skirt," she'll say, or, "This isn't the right sweater." She cries as school time approaches, and on Friday she refuses lunch and the clothes change. So Robin asks Desiree's dad why clothes are so important.

"She loves nice clothes so we let her select what she wants to wear. She does well," Desiree's dad says.

"Apparently, though," Robin says, "she's worrying about making the wrong choices."

"Tonight we're going shopping, and she gets to choose a new coat," he says.

"How will I know what coat to buy?" Desiree asks, beginning to cry.

"Oh, honey," her dad says tenderly drying her tears. To Robin he says, "Thanks. We are expecting too much too soon!"

Kids are fortunate to have you to put balance into their lives when expectations get beyond what they can handle.

The motto should not be: Forgive one another; rather, Understand one another.

— EMMA GOLDMAN

Stella uses my rented child care room to teach Sunday school. Sharing space with her is difficult. She believes mothers should stay home with their children and she is messy. Monday I found dried-up markers, dolls in the block area, and seashells in the toy stove. So on Sunday I went to see Stella. The calm scene surprised me. Music hummed as the children played. Stella gave gentle hugs. She didn't notice that they were undoing my perfect classroom.

"Clean up," she said. "Other people use our room and we should leave it nice for them."

Stella saw me. "Oh, hi! Aren't the children great?" she asked me. "I'd love to talk but I'm off to visit my sister's kids. She died in a car accident on her way home from work two years ago, you know."

"No, I'm sorry," I said. "I didn't know."

You support others who care for children. You appreciate their strengths and weaknesses, understanding that there is always more than one point of view.

Your world is as big as you make it.

— GEORGIA DOUGLAS JOHNSON

Looking up from helping a toddler in her fenced yard, Blanche sees a small child across the street, clumsily carrying a blanket, about to step onto the busy thoroughfare.

"Oh, my!" Blanche gasps, moving quickly out the gate and locking it behind her. While the child waits for a traffic break, Blanche weaves her way through, holding up her hand to slow oncoming cars.

Reaching the child, she asks, "Sweetie, where's mommy?"

"She resting. I going walking," the child answers.

Blanche scoops up blanket and child, crosses the street, and calls the local police. Three hours later, a frantic young mother arrives, explaining that she naps when her child does and leaves for her night job after dinner when her husband takes over.

"It scares me that I didn't hear her leave," she says.

Blanche offers a cup of tea and arranges to have the two year old stay with her while her mom gets some daytime rest.

The importance of your caring is rarely more apparent than when it's lacking for children wanting to expand their world.

Love is or it ain't. Thin love ain't love at all.

— TONI MORRISON

Selma had an armful of egg cartons for the recycling bin. Not able to see where she was going, she bumped into a shelf.

Crash! The terrarium hit the floor and formed a clump of muddy soil, glass, and broken green plants.

"Uh oh!" Selma called out. "Hao, we need you!"

"Boy, oh boy, are you in big trouble," Sia, a new five year old, said. "Wait until she sees this mess. You'll be on a time out for the rest of your life."

Selma said. "Hao's cool."

Hao came, carrying a broom, dustpan, and wastebasket. "We have some work to do here."

"I'll be more careful next time," Selma said. "It was an accident."

"It sure isn't anything you'd want to do on purpose," Hao said. "Let's get busy."

Selma grabbed the broom and smiled at Sia, "Cool, definitely, cool."

You put love and security in children's lives where others have tried to plant fear and shame. Kids know that through thick and thin your love for them just is.

The best gifts are always tied with heartstrings.

— ELIZABETH BIBESCO

The lights are dimmed in the YMCA auditorium. On stage, the spotlight is on Francine, Jess, and their four-year-old son, Jason, who will be presenting his home care provider, Beth Kelly, with the "Caregiver of the Year Award."

"Beth is a second mother, a teacher, a role model, and a security blanket," Francine says. "She's made our little boy feel right at home. She has taught him to play games and to tell stories, and the other kids how to converse with him.

"She is helping us raise an independent, productive, well-adjusted child. She's taken two night courses during her precious time off to do that and has taught the other kids what she's learned," Jess adds.

Together they say, "Most of all she's given him friendship."

The spotlight then includes Jason and four other preschoolers who join him on stage. Soundlessly, five small pairs of hands sign their message to Beth, "Thank you, for helping us be friends."

You give the gift of caring from the heart to all children who have that special need for love.

Crisis changes people and turns ordinary people into
wiser or more responsible ones.

— WILMA P. MANKILLER

Years ago, Marna marched for women and
attended civil rights rallies. Since then, she's been
caring for kids—making their lives better. When a
local company began dumping toxic waste into
the water, she got involved again. She wrote letters
and lobbied legislators. Nothing changed so she
joined a group of concerned citizens who blocked
the entrances to the company building and
got arrested.

Marna went to court. In her testimony she said,
"I want to say to children that I did everything that
I could to make the world safe for them. That I
noticed. That I cared." The court sent her to jail
for a few days.

When Marna returned, a parent told her, "I'm
looking for a new job. I work for that company that
you stood up against. I want my kids to know how
much I care too. Thanks for the courage."

You stand up for children every day by being
responsible for their well-being. You inspire
others to take children seriously, to act for them
courageously, and to tend to them lovingly.

Snowflakes, leaves, humans, plants, raindrops,
stars, molecules, microscopic entities all come in
communities. The singular cannot in reality exist.

— PAULA GUNN ALLEN

Cranberry juice streamed down the table
and dripped onto the floor. Sally lowered her
head. Spilling things seemed to be her specialty.
Embarrassed, she walked slowly to get the cleanup
bucket. When she got back to the table, three of
her friends pitched in and helped her wipe up the
red stuff. Kneeling next to Sally, Gregory said in
a hushed tone, "Don't worry, that's what friends
are for."

You teach children that things go better when
people work together. Your lessons will help make
the communities of the future better places to live.

If we had no winter, the spring would not be so pleasant.
— ANNE BRADSTREET

The preschoolers have decorated the playroom with paper flowers they've made. Later they'll have cake with candles because Jason is coming back. The two year old had been in infant care at the center, but at age eleven months he developed what doctors treated as a recurring viral ear infection until they discovered Jason's cancer.

"Will we sing 'Happy Birthday' to him?" Suzanne asks.

"No, it's not his birthday. We'll sing other songs," the teacher says.

"Then, why are we having candles?" Suzanne asks.

"Because we want Jason's party to shine," the teacher answers, tying two shimmering silver "Welcome Back" balloons to a high chair.

"Nothing we've experienced has been more chilling than Jason's illness," the director tells a helping parent. "When that recovered little boy toddles in here today, it will be spring after a long, dark winter."

Through their dreariest of winters, your caring gives kids the hope of spring.

She who laughs, lasts.

— MARY PETTIBONE POOLE

Glenda is the chair of the neighborhood association. At the last meeting, she had the group laughing, as usual, as she told about the little girl who threw all of the mittens into the toilet.

"Glena, I don't know how you do it," Debbie, a new member, chuckled. "Seventeen years in the business and still laughing"

"Correction, eighteen years. And that's how I do it, laughing."

You learned long ago to laugh at the small stuff so that you can handle the big stuff. Your ability to laugh is one of the reasons you are so good at what you do.

If you see your work as a mission, the world expects dedication for which you shouldn't expect money.

— MARGARET BOYER

"If the world made sense," the seminar leader tells the child care providers, "the nursery school teacher would rank higher than the typical college professor. She (the teacher almost invariably is a she) would be selected with better care, trained more thoroughly, and paid a higher salary than instructors at higher levels. That's a statement from an article in a child psychologists' magazine from 1968.

"When T-shirts that read 'I haven't sat on a baby yet' are standard apparel for a gathering like this, we know that in the 1990's we're far from the world we envision.

"But quality child care remains our mission, quality pay our goal, dedication our weapon. Success will be not our dream, but our reality."

When you insist that the world value child care, you take on a mission and courageously reach out to the future for the children on whom it depends.

You have to know that your real home is within.

— QUINCY JONES

Wiping sleep out of his eyes, three-year-old Blaine plops one stumbling foot next to the other.

"He fell asleep on the way over," his dad whispers, as he walks past the morning circle time. "I'll give him some time to wake up." He takes Blaine into the other room.

"There's the porcelain pitcher," Blaine yawns.

"Right," his dad says. "Do you want me to pour you some juice?"

"I will," Blaine answers. "You can go now, Dad, I'm safe."

The comfortable and loving place that you provide for children allows them to feel safe, confident, and at home with themselves.

*When you have only two pennies left in the world,
buy a loaf of bread with one and a lily with the other.*

— CHINESE PROVERB

He is a tall man wearing an overcoat with frayed cuffs and worn fur collar, torn knit gloves, and cap. He has collected his two children from the evening child care center and waits with them in the unheated office building entrance for their mom, who works on the cleanup crew.

The kids, about ages two and three, warmly dressed in new hooded parkas, eagerly open their fast-food kiddie packs. Delightedly, they unwrap the kid-sized cheeseburgers and munch on fries. Dad opens their juice cartons, and says, "Enjoy."

Later, he picks up their empty bags, cartons, and wrappers, and takes two small stuffed dinosaurs from his pocket, a surprise that has the kids jumping happily.

Some passersby smile. Some comment critically to one another, "Just what they need—dinosaurs." Their dad stoops to accept their hugs and, arms enfolding them, savors their love.

Thank you for persevering for children and supporting parents who know that kids do, indeed, need dinosaurs.

DECEMBER 6

Those who are responsible for the soul food of children are wise to clean out their refrigerators frequently.

— TRACY E. P. STELTEN

Someone spilled apple juice in the refrigerator and didn't clean it up. I discovered it when it was sticky brown slime on the bottom shelf.

"I know who's to blame for this," I said to myself. "Those schoolagers. Gary lets them come in here, use the fridge, get things out of the cupboard. I'm sick of it."

When I went into the back storeroom to get the preschool snack, I heard the schoolagers lumbering in. Gary chatted with kids about their day at school.

One child said, "Can I get anybody a glass of juice? How about some crackers and cheese?"

"Count me in," said another child and added with a sigh, "Geez, it's great to be home."

"There's no place like it," I mused. "But we can try. We can try."

You feed the souls of kids when you allow them to become independent, confident people, even if means things get a little messy.

Happiness itself is a kind of gratitude.

— JOSEPH WOOD KRUTCH

The kids in Margaret's care lie in the park snow, fanning out arms and legs, making snow angels. They get up, wave at the school bus passing by, and run to slide down the high snow banks along the road.

The temperature is 25 degrees Fahrenheit, so after an hour Margaret says, "Let's go. Don't want anyone to get too cold."

Leaving, she hears a child crying and stops to listen. Jennifer, running out ahead, calls back, "Someone's in this snow bank."

They all dig and Margaret lifts out frightened six-year-old Todd. The school bus had left him near his house across the park, but he had decided to scale the banks before going home. Margaret brushes him off as his panicked mother approaches, shouting, "Have you seen a little boy?"

Todd runs to her. His mother hugs him over and over again and carries him away. Jennifer looks at Margaret and says, "She didn't say thank you."

"But, honey, look at how happy she is," Margaret replies.

You are a role model for little people who learn from you that the happiness of others is a satisfying reward for caring.

Never let the pain in your heart drown the song in your soul.

— MALIK DEL MALIK

"Hush, little baby, don't say a word," Ia sang to six-month-old Willy. Her body rocked back and forth gently to her own music as Willy's feathery black eyelashes sleepily fluttered and then closed. She carried the flannel-wrapped bundle to his bed, laid him down, and brushed light circles on Willy's back with her strong hands.

Hannah watched from the hallway. When Ia approached, Hannah held out her hand and gave her friend a tender squeeze.

"Ia," Hannah said, "if it is too difficult for you to take care of babies so soon after your miscarriage, we can work something else out."

"No, no. Listening to the songs in these babies' souls helps my wounded heart heal," Ia said, gently returning her friend's hand hug.

On days when your heart is heavy with worries or sadness, let the children help you remember the music in your soul.

If you feel like a winner, you act like a winner.

— CINDY BELONGIA

Joey's in trouble for truancy, and the police officer leaves him with Barbara, a counselor at the juvenile detention center. The boy spews obscenities at her while she calls his grandmother.

Distraught, his grandma arrives. "His daddy sent him to live with me so he'd get into a good school," she says. "But the other kids have been hard on him. I work, so he's alone after school; and he's been hanging with a gang of bigger kids who don't want him. He's only seven."

When Joey sees his grandma, the toughness melts and tears come. Grandma, arms around him, says, "Straighten up and be proud. Remember what I told you to tell yourself when people try to make you feel like you ain't nobody?"

Joey nods but his grandma says, "Tell me."

Head down, he begins, "I know I'm somebody . . ." his grandma puts her hand under his chin, lifts his head, while he continues, ". . . 'cause God don't make no junk!"

You make kids into winners when you see beyond their facades to the children they are; children who need your support and understanding.

We should never get too tired or too sophisticated to march.

— MARTIN LUTHER KING, SR.

It was a blowy, blustery day—too cold for the preschoolers at Marion Elementary to go outside. The four year olds looked out the window and sighed. "Another day stuck in here," a child complained.

"Cheer up," the teacher said. "Let's have a parade." He passed out the shakers, bells, and tambourines.

"Now get those knees up and let's march. Remember our song: 'We are marching for a better world, a better world.'"

Clanking down the halls, the miniband caused quite a stir among the classroom teachers who complained to the principal.

To their surprise, the principal announced, "Okay, everybody. Get on those marching shoes and join our little friends. We could all use a better world, don't you think?"

From you, children learn how to make a weary day hopeful. Sometimes they can even get others to sing along.

Everything else you grow out of, but you never recover from childhood.

— BERYL BAINBRIDGE

The four year olds play in the housekeeping corner at Kelsey's family child care home. Patrice puts a baby doll in its cradle and says, "I took her for a walk, and the fresh air made her sleepy."

"Sorry I'm late getting home, but the meeting went over time and I had to get Jimmy from child care," Sandra says. "I'll start dinner."

Tony enters and says, "Isn't supper ready? I've gotta go bowling. We don't need vegetables. I'll just fix some hot dogs."

He nudges Sandra away from the sink and attempts to take the cooking pot out of her hand. Sheila and Patrice, stepping out of their make-believe roles, say loudly, "You're not the boss!"

Tony looks at them with an expression that says, "I don't understand," and then softly replies with an incredulous voice, "But I'm the dad!"

Adult behavior indelibly marks the hearts of kids. Much you can't control, but your gentle fairness gives them choices to make as they grow away from childhood.

How we spend our days is how we spend our lives.

— ANNIE DILLARD

"Bang, bang, you're dead!" Chris shot Frank with his Tinkertoy gun.

"Remember what Mrs. Jergens says?" Frank said. "We don't want to practice hurting people."

Kids hear you when you spend your days teaching them how to spend their lives.

Who takes the child by the hand takes the mother by the heart.

— DANISH PROVERB

Lynn, a child care provider, and Roxanne, mother of two-and-a-half-year-old Bonnie, discuss plans for the new baby expected in five weeks. Roxanne and her husband, Bill, are from out of state and have no family nearby.

"My mother will come and stay for a month," says Roxanne, "but I'm thrilled that you'll take Bonnie and the baby afterward. It means so much to me."

Roxanne and Bonnie leave. With the last of her child care brood gone, Lynn whips up a dessert, readies her house for company, and at 8 p.m. is greeting her guests at the door. The phone rings; it's Roxanne.

"Lynn, I'm so sorry to bother you, but the baby's coming. Please, could we bring Bonnie to you?" she asks anxiously.

"Of course," Lynn answers. Within thirty minutes, the car is in the driveway. Bill lifts Bonnie from her car seat, reaches for a small bag, and turns to see his child already running up the walk toward Lynn who takes the delighted Bonnie inside.

You comfort someone's heart each time you lovingly take a child into your own.

To love means you also trust.

— JOAN BAEZ

Tanya, an aide in the preschool room, watches three-year-old Delmar drawing.

"The snow in your pictures is always purple. That's very interesting," she says.

"It looks really shiny and sparkly that way," responds Delmar, tilting his head and studying his picture.

"Yes, it is beautiful," says Tanya, admiring the new sparkles she sees in the snow.

Because you love and respect them, children are not afraid to share their world with you. Helping children to trust themselves is one of the greatest gifts you give.

A good laugh is sunshine in a house.

— WILLIAM THACKERAY

Randy is a five-year-old curly-headed little guy who walks with a swagger and talks with a southwest Iowa twang. He's in kindergarten in the morning and in Janice's child care home in the afternoon. He says he wants to be an astronaut when he grows up and ride a rocket to the moon. Full of energy, he resists the after-lunch rest periods.

Yesterday, when Randy was disturbing kids trying to rest, Janice whispered to him, "You know what I'm going to do with you?"

"No. What?" Randy drawled.

"I'm going to send you to the moon," she whispered.

"Oh, good!" said Randy, and Janice added, "The shiny, slippery, sliding side."

Randy loved that. He sat upright in the middle of his nap mat, clutched his toes and doubled over with laughter, but finally settled down.

He nodded off, repeatedly trying to say, without stumbling, "The shiny, slippery, sliding side."

You change stressful moments to fun times because you know how to make children laugh.

*The elders say, 'The longest road you're going to have
to walk in your life is . . . from the head to the heart.'
But they also say that you can't speak to the people
as a leader unless you've made the return journey.
From the heart back to the head.*

— PHIL LANE, JR.

When seven-year-old Nin died of AIDS, Ann, her teacher, sat with her little sister, Allie, and their mother, both of whom also have the disease.

"Is she gone?" Allie asked.

"Yes," her mother said.

"Mommy, can I die when you do?"

Ann's heart wept on the long subway ride home.

A week later, Ann bravely told the sad story to a grant-giving board in a glassy skyscraper. People cried openly.

"I'm sure your tears are real," she said, "but your dollars will give children what they need to help them heal. Please think about it. Thank you."

You are the voice for children when they can't speak for themselves. Continue to be brave in your heart and your head. You are a true leader.

Light tomorrow with today!

— Elizabeth Barrett Browning

Ada steps inside Felicia's family child care home, sets down a large gift-wrapped box, pulls off her cap and scarf, and catches two-year-old Keith who comes running.

"For me, Auntie?" Keith asks, reaching for the box.

"For you," Ada says.

While he tears into the wrapping, Ada explains to Felicia, "His birthday is next week, but he needs this today."

Keith pulls out boots, a jacket, cap, and mittens.

"Let's see if they fit," Ada says.

"They fit," Keith tells her.

Everything is slightly large, but once on, Keith refuses to part with any of it. He runs back to where the other kids are playing and sits, legs outstretched, admiring his boots.

"He doesn't get many new things," Ada apologizes. "I'm on my lunch hour. Can I leave without getting him out of this get up?"

"Oh, sure," Felicia says. "It's a thrill to see him so happy."

Ada blows a kiss and leaves Keith stroking his jacket sleeves, joy on his face.

Your day-to-day caring has earned you the moments that lift your heart when someone brightens a child's tomorrow.

What are we doing here? We're reaching for the stars.
— CHRISTA MCAULIFFE

Mia, Crystal, and Ginger glued bead designs. The six year olds' conversation included, "What are you going to be when you grow up?" Their after-school teacher, Dorothy, pulled up a chair. The girls wanted to be hair stylists, teachers, and artists.

"Those are all neat things to do," Dorothy said. "What do you think you can't be?"

"President," Crystal answered quickly, "'cause it's against the law."

"No, it's not," Dorothy said.

"For sure?"

"For sure!"

"Well, then, out of my way! I'm going to be Crystal, President of the United States!"

"Could be. It could be," Dorothy nodded.

You open new worlds to children and put their stars within reach. You may help change history. It could be.

It may be those who do most dream most.

In the gym, Josh dribbles, shoots, and practices his slam dunk. He commentates as he goes, reporting play by play on a basketball game in which he's the star. But what he really wants is to teach computer science.

"He's a dreamer," his mom says with a grin, "like me." She had followed her dream from a Chicago project, where gunfire was a daily threat, to a safer place for her three boys.

Josh is the oldest, a sixth grader. He's also a baseball history buff, with heroes like Casey Stengel, coach of seven pennant-winning teams, and Jackie Robinson, the first black major league player.

His mom works two jobs and depends on after-school care for the boys. She watches the ball beat a steady rhythm under Josh's guiding hand and murmurs, "Yes, Josh, we're dreamers, you and me."

When you encourage kids to dream, you give them hope and help make this world a better place to be.

To light a candle is to cast a shadow.

— URSULA K. LE GUIN

Sherry darkened the room except for one shining light. Finger shadows stretched along the wall as the kids' hands formed ducks, rabbits, and other shadow puppets that starred in short plays.

"What do you want to be when you grow up, little duck?" the dark bunny asked.

"Same thing as I am today," answered the finger-powered duck, "an absolutely awesome person, or I mean duck."

You light up children's lives with creativity. The sense of self-worth that you give them will guide them through life's shadow days.

Stand up for yourself and you'll stand up for children.

— MARGARET BOYER

As Janine and Sam slowly make their way into the auditorium, amid two hundred or so child care professionals, they laugh at the humor in the Alliance Conference brochure.

"Why did the child care worker cross the road?" Janine asks.

Sam reads the answer, "To get to her other job."

"How about this one?" he says, "What is nine dollars an hour?"

Janine reads, "What child care workers would love to earn, and a public school teacher would refuse to work for."

"And," Janine asks, "What two things in a child care worker's life are itsy-bitsy?"

Together they laugh, "A spider and a paycheck."

"Ain't that the truth, though," Sam laughs as they settle into their seats, determined to work for improved salaries and working conditions in the profession they love.

You do the world's most important work, and you stand up for children, whenever you rise to your feet to say so.

The ribbon of love is a dream worth holding on to.

— JANE EVERSHED

Layon, a funny, feisty six year old, died. She ran into the mall parking lot while her mother took a brief second to check for her keys. A car hit her. It wasn't anyone's fault, it was simply tragic. Her friends missed her very much. Their teacher, Faye, tried to help them. One day, she had the children pass a long, bright green ribbon around a circle. They could say something about Layon or be silent and remember her.

Jessica, her best friend, spoke last. Clutching the ribbon she said, "In my dreams, Layon laughs. Then I don't feel the hole in my heart."

After class, Faye gave the ribbon to Jessica. "Hold on to this when you miss Layon. Maybe it will help your heartache a little."

You give kids something to hold on to when they are lonely and sad. When you believe in their dreams, you teach them about the power of love and hope.

Every time a bell rings, an angel gets his wings.
                              — IT'S A WONDERFUL LIFE

He is six years old and telling his story on television. He wears his favorite oversized sweatshirt and jeans and wears his baseball cap, front to back. A typical kid except he has only weeks, perhaps days, to live because of cancer.

He tells the TV interviewer he is lucky. His caregivers, nurses, doctors, and his mom say he gets to go to heaven a lot sooner than they will.

"When I get there," the boy says, "I want to be my mom's guardian angel."

His mom reaches for his hand and says, mistily, "I'm going to miss him."

Whether your caring reaches out to healthy children or you walk among the ill—soothing, supporting, preparing them for whatever comes—you're earning your wings.

We give and take with no line in between.

— MARGE PIERCY

Her small brown fingers curl around my thumb.

"Hush, little baby," I hum.

She smiles one of those baby smiles that pulls you in, wraps you up, and takes the rest of the world away.

Gently I rock her and feel her little body relax.

Cooing, she snuggles into my chest, just fitting into the curves of my arm.

"I love you, baby. And I know that you love me, too."

The love you share with children is a give and take. That love is filled with warmth and trust that only those who cherish children have the good fortune to understand. It is a beautiful life.

The giving of love is an education in itself.

— ELEANOR ROOSEVELT

Addie, the preschool teacher, is working a puzzle with three-year-old Tomica when Tomica's mom arrives to take her home. Tomica gives Addie a hug, shakes a small finger at her, and says, "I have to go, but don't you be lonesome."

"Addie's my teacher," she tells her mom. When Tomica turns to wave good-bye, she sees Addie helping Travis with the puzzle she left behind. Tomica breaks away from her mom, runs to the puzzle, scatters it to the floor, and pushes at Travis. "She's my teacher, not yours," Tomica cries.

Addie holds Tomica on her lap and says, "Travis needs a teacher too. How would you feel if you didn't have a teacher at all?"

"Bad," Tomica says.

"That's how Travis feels. What can we do?" Addie asks.

Tomica thinks a while, then slides off Addie's lap. "You can be his teacher too," she says to Addie. But while running toward her mom, she adds, "Till I get back."

You give children an education in love as you teach them to solve problems by caring and sharing.

Wild women don't worry; they don't have no blues.

— IDA COX

The women spin around, dancing to the beat of the music. It is the end of a long day. They have come from all over the state. Some hired subs, others lost income to be here. Today they raged, cried, and strategized with each other as they shared stories of families who are cold at night and hungry in the morning.

Tomorrow, with petitions in hand from people back home, they go to tell their stories to legislators—to see if they can get money for child care and training programs. But tonight they are whirling, twirling, singing in one strong voice, and not getting the blues.

When you sign a petition, go to the statehouse, or put in a good day's work caring for children, you join others in making things better. After all of that, you deserve to kick up your heels once in a while!

It has begun to occur to me that life is a stage I'm going through.

— ELLEN GOODMAN

Tony throws a tantrum at Carol's child care home. "No! Carol do!" he cries when his dad insists on helping him with his jacket.

"Come on, you little rug rat," his dad says playfully. "He does this at home if my wife's around. He'll say, 'Mommy do.' Where do I come in?"

"Just wait." Carol says, taking the jacket. "He's only two and a half. From seven until the teens, Dad's the hero. I don't support the 'terrible twos' theory. But we like labels from 'rug rats' to 'teenagers' to 'thirtysomethings' to 'yuppies' or whatever on to 'goldenagers.' I'd go along with 'terrific twos.'"

"Hey, kid, see ya when you're seven," Tony's dad says. To Carol, he adds, "You made me feel a lot better about this. I guess you saw it was getting to me. I even accused my wife of encouraging it. So, thanks."

Hoisting Tony to his shoulder, he says, "Let's go see Mommy."

Your knowledge of child development makes parents feel less worried and defensive as they cope with their children's changing behaviors.

I want to be all I'm capable of becoming.

— KATHERINE MANSFIELD

The after-school kids bound off the buses. They jostle, bump each other, head for the hall, drop their backpacks, hurry into the lavatories, race to the snack bar.

Some head for the gym to hear rules for a kickball game—eight-year-old Matt among them. He listens, bright-eyed and eager, for about five minutes. Then he begins to squirm, looks around, and elbows the kid next to him, who brushes him off with a slap at his arm. The elbowing becomes punching. Kids around hiss, "Cut it out!"

Jeremy, the teacher's aide, steps quietly in behind Matt. "Remember, Matt, be calm. Be calm," he says. Matt works hard, gets himself under control, and stays.

Your understanding of kids with ADD (attention deficit syndrome) helps them become all they're capable of being, knowing they don't struggle alone.

Each year is a sort of graduation, with all of us moving a step ahead within our own history.

— JUDITH A. KIRKWOOD

"Tomorrow is the end of another year, and what do I have to show for it?" Janella asked herself as she wiped supper's spaghetti sauce off the stove.

"All I do is take care of kids, raise a family, go to school (hopefully someday I will graduate), volunteer at the homeless shelter, chair the legislative committee for the Child Care Association, listen to my friends, and sing in the synagogue."

She poured herself a cup of peppermint tea and watched the snow gliding in the glistening winter air.

"Hey, that's a pretty long list. I might not make the history books, but I just might make a difference," she thought as she headed upstairs to check on her kids.

You moved ahead this year while helping others to do the same. Congratulations on graduating and stepping into the new year with a sense of your own purpose and history.

We end this year with hearts full of gratitude for all of the talented good people whose stories, strengths, and struggles fill this book. We think it fitting that the last reading for this year comes from a child care worker and poet.

We sow the seeds on the other side of the water,
and never see the harvest turn to flower.
Yet we dance in the colors of the day
and know the power of the bursting bud.

We teach the children to sing
Though we will hear the song but faintly
Falling away across the water.
And the loud applause
will not sound for us
Only the soft stirrings of peace
in the children's hearts
And the thunder of the ages in their veins.

— LINDA RHODY

We are a richer people and our world is a stronger, more compassionate place because you dedicate yourself to the love of children. Peace.

INDEX

ABOUT THE AUTHORS

Jean Steiner and Mary Steiner Whelan are a mother and daughter from the Minneapolis-St. Paul area. Jean has worked as a home child care provider, a college writing instructor, and director of the Minnesota House of Representatives Public Information Program. Mary's experience encompasses nearly all areas of early childhood education. She is a trainer, a diversity consultant, a manager for Redleaf Press, and an activist for peace and social justice.